Why Stay Alive?

Searching for an Anchor When Life Implodes

Aham Igbokwe

Why Stay Alive?

Searching for an Anchor When Life Implodes

Copyright © 2026 Ahamefule Igbokwe

The composite characters and illustrative vignettes in this book are fictional constructions drawn from documented patterns of human experience. They do not represent, depict, or refer to any specific person, living or dead.

This book discusses suicide, suicidal feelings, and mental health crises. It is not a substitute for professional care. If you or someone you know is in distress, please get in touch with a crisis service in your country.

International crisis supports resources:

www.findahelpline.com — a global directory of crisis lines by country

www.befrienders.org — worldwide emotional support network

www.iasp.info — International Association for Suicide Prevention

www.samaritans.org—the charity that prevents suicide

www.papyrus-uk.org —prevention of suicide amongst young people

www.thecalmzone.net —suicide prevention with emphasis on men

ISBN (Paperback): 978-1-918518-16-0
ISBN (eBook): 978-1-918518-15-3

First Edition

Cover design: @IamPastorAham
Interior design and typesetting: @IamPastorAham

Dedication

To those still inside it, and

To those who stay close enough to matter.

Epigraph

The thought of suicide is a great consolation: by means of it, one gets through many a night.

— Friedrich Nietzsche

Contents

Author's Note

This book began as a question I could not avoid.

Not a theoretical question. Not a philosophical exercise. A question that arrived — and kept arriving — from inside a life that, by most visible measures, was functioning well. Career intact. Relationships present. Faith active. And yet, underneath all of it, something that did not respond to any of those things.

I have lived with what I would describe as the *feeling* of being suicidal — not the thought of it, but the feeling. The distinction may seem subtle. It is not. Suicidal thoughts involve conscious consideration — a cognitive process that can, in principle, be challenged, redirected, or treated. What I have experienced is different: an emotional state. A weight. A consuming pressure that does not argue or reason, and therefore cannot easily be argued or reasoned with. It simply presses.

For years, I could not find language for this. The clinical world had categories that did not quite fit. The faith world had answers that did not quite reach. And so, the question persisted, quietly, beneath a life that continued regardless.

This book is my attempt to investigate that question seriously — not to resolve it cheaply or to shield the reader from its full weight. I wanted to follow the question wherever it led, examine every anchor that human beings have reached for when life implodes, and be honest about what holds and what does not.

I write as someone still inside that investigation. Not as someone who has arrived.

If you are reading this from inside your own version of the question, I want you to know that professional care — therapy, clinical support, honest conversation with a doctor — is not a retreat from the search. It is often what makes the search survivable. I say that not as a disclaimer, but as someone who has needed it.

What follows is not a survival manual. It is not a self-help programme. *It is an honest attempt to find out whether there is something real enough to hold onto when everything else gives way.*

I will be honest with you from the outset: I am not writing from the other side of this. This book is not my testimony of rescue. It is, in the most literal sense, my search — a last-ditch, serious attempt to find out whether an anchor actually exists. Whether anything is real and strong enough to hold when everything else gives way.

If it does exist, I intend to find it. And I want to find it honestly — not by settling for comfort, but by following the question wherever it leads.

That is where Chapter One begins.

—*Ahamefule Igbokwe*
Berkshire, United Kingdom

CHAPTER 1 — *When Life Implodes*

There are moments in life when things do not simply go wrong.

They collapse. Not always dramatically. Not always visibly. Not always in ways others can recognise.

But something inside gives way. And when it does, life never feels the same again.

What makes this collapse difficult to explain is that, from the outside, nothing may appear broken. A person can still have plans for the future, laugh and smile, appear composed, maintain a career, speak positively, support others, show up and get things done. They may even have had a happy childhood, been surrounded by friends and family, expressed gratitude, and appeared strong.

And yet, internally, something is not right.

Mental distress does not always announce itself in visible ways. It can exist quietly beneath functionality, productivity, and outward stability. A person may continue to live as though normal while internally struggling to understand why they are still living at all.

For some, this struggle does not even take the form of clear thoughts.

It is not always *"I want to die."*

Sometimes it is far less defined — and far more difficult to explain.

It is a feeling. A persistent, heavy, consuming emotional weight. William Styron, writing from inside a severe depressive episode, described it not as sadness but as a kind of *brainstorm* — a tempest in the brain that bore no relationship to ordinary unhappiness. [1] That distinction is important. Because it points toward something many people who suffer in this way already know but struggle to articulate: the experience is not primarily about thought. It is about being overtaken.

In my own experience, the struggle has not primarily been about thinking of ending my life, but about feeling overwhelmed by something I could not always name or explain. A kind of emotional encasement. A pressure that does not argue or reason — it simply presses. At times, intensely. At times, persistently. At times, without warning.

The feeling is not new. I can trace it, now, to a young man living alone in Port Harcourt — an engineer in his bachelorhood years, more than seventeen years before any clinical diagnosis would arrive to name what was already present. I remember the bouts of it with a vividness that time has not reduced. Not thoughts. Not plans. But a feeling — specific and recurring — that I wished the earth were flat, so I could keep walking until I dropped off the edge. There was no violence in the image. No destination. Only the wish for a continuation that eventually ran out. A walking that went on long enough to be relieved of the burden of turning back. I had no language for it then. I have more now. But the experience the language is trying to reach is the same one that arrived, unnamed and unexplained, in a young man in Port Harcourt who had none of the frameworks this book will examine — and who carried it, quietly, for decades before any of them were available to him.

A state that feels less like a decision, and more like weather moving through.

This distinction matters.

Because not all despair is cognitive, some of it is deeply emotional. [2] When despair is emotional rather than logical, it becomes harder to address. There is no clear argument to challenge. No defined thought to dismantle. Only a weight to endure — and, at its worst, to survive.

It is worth saying plainly: people who experience this kind of sustained emotional distress benefit from professional care. Not because the distress is weakness, but because its nature makes it resistant to the usual remedies of will, perspective, and time.

In such moments, life does not necessarily feel unbearable because of one specific problem. It feels unbearable because everything seems to lose coherence at once. Meaning becomes unclear. Effort feels disconnected from the outcome. Hope feels distant — or even unrealistic. Each day is discharged rather than lived. The passage of time becomes its own particular grief: not because things are getting worse, but because they are not getting better, and the waiting has become its own kind of suffering.

And when meaning begins to dissolve, a question begins to form.

Not loudly at first. Not even consciously. But steadily.

Why continue living?

This question is often avoided. It is considered uncomfortable. Dangerous, even. So, it is suppressed, redirected, or quickly answered with familiar reassurances: *Things will get better. Stay positive. Focus on what you have.*

These responses, while well-intentioned, often do not go to the heart of the question.

Because the question is not always about circumstances, it is about meaning.

When life implodes — whether suddenly or gradually — the issue is no longer how to cope, improve, or endure. The issue becomes more fundamental:

Why continue to live at all?

For some, this question appears briefly and disappears. For others, it lingers. And for some, it becomes unavoidable.

It is important to say this clearly: the presence of this question does not make a person weak. It does not make them ungrateful. It does not make them spiritually diminished. It means they have encountered something that many people spend their lives avoiding.

The collapse of assumed meaning.

Up to a certain point, life is often carried by assumptions — that things will work out, that effort will be rewarded, that meaning will naturally emerge. These assumptions are rarely examined. They operate, quietly, beneath the surface of daily life. And most of the time, they suffice.

But when they break, something deeper is required. Not a distraction. Not temporary relief. Not borrowed positivity. But something structurally capable of holding when everything else does not.

Viktor Frankl, who survived Auschwitz and went on to build an entire field of psychological inquiry around the subject, observed that the person who has a *'why'* to live can bear almost any *how*. [3] It is a remark that has outlived its century because it names something people in extremity recognise as true — not philosophically, but in the body. In the moment.

The search for that *why* is what this book is about.

Not as an intellectual exercise. Not as a philosophical hobby. But as something far more urgent.

A search for an anchor. Something that is not dependent on circumstances, success, emotional fluctuation, or external validation. Something that can hold even when life does not hold.

This book does not begin with that anchor already defined.

It begins here.

At the point where life has imploded and no longer makes sense to continue, at the point where the question can no longer be ignored.

Why stay alive?

That is the question. And from here, the search begins.

CHAPTER 2 — *When Despair Takes Different Forms*

There is a particular kind of confusion that surrounds mental suffering — and it begins with the assumption that despair, when serious enough, will make itself known.

That it will announce itself in recognisable ways. That the person experiencing it will be visibly struggling, clearly distressed, or at a minimum, able to say what is wrong.

This assumption is understandable. It is also, in many cases, wrong.

Consider someone who still shows up to work. Still speaks clearly. Still fulfils responsibilities. Still laughs at the right moments. If you encountered them briefly, you would have no reason to worry. From the outside, nothing appears broken.

But internally, something is happening that does not match the outward picture.

There are no plans to die. No rehearsed thoughts. No careful consideration of ending life. And yet there is a persistent, overwhelming sense that something is deeply wrong — not with a particular situation or a specific person, but with life itself. A kind of enclosure. An invisible pressure. Not sharp enough to name, not logical enough to argue with, but heavy enough to alter the texture of everyday.

I know this particular room from the inside.

In my own experience, the struggle has rarely taken the form people expect. It has not been a matter of thinking about ending my life, but of feeling persistently overwhelmed by something I could not always interpret. There was no clear narrative — only a state. No argument to win or lose — only a weight to carry.

This matters because what people typically look for are signals that they can read: *Are you thinking about suicide? Do you have a plan? What exactly is wrong?* These are reasonable questions. But they are calibrated to detect one particular form of despair. And despair, it turns out, does not arrive in only one form.

The First Form: Feeling

The psychologist Edwin Shneidman spent decades studying what drives people toward suicide and concluded that the primary engine was not thought but pain — what he called *psychache*: an unbearable psychological suffering that demands relief. [1] It was a radical reframing, because it shifted the focus from cognition to experience. From *what a person thinks* to *what a person feels*.

This form of despair is not primarily ideational. It does not present as a plan or a wish or even a clearly articulable thought. It presents as a state — an experience of deep sadness, emptiness, agitation, or heaviness that does not resolve through reasoning, because it was never generated by reasoning in the first place.

Someone in this state may say, if asked: *I'm not thinking about suicide.* And they would be telling the truth. What they might not be able to say — because the language barely exists for it — is: *I cannot bear how these feel. And I do not know why it feels this way.*

That second sentence is not a failure of insight. It is an accurate description of the experience. The absence of a reason is part of the suffering.

The Second Form: Thought

For others, despair takes a more structured shape. It appears as cognition — as thought that can be traced, described, and in some cases, planned.

This might include passive wishes such as *"I wish I could disappear,"* intrusive images of death, imagined scenarios of escape, or, in more severe presentations, active planning. This form is more visible to clinicians and to the people around the sufferer, because it produces language. It can be named, tracked, and addressed through therapeutic intervention. [2]

The cognitive form is not necessarily more dangerous than the emotional form. But it is more legible — and that legibility has shaped most of our clinical and cultural frameworks for understanding suicidal crisis.

The Overlap

Many people experience both emotional weight and intermittent thought, sometimes simultaneously, sometimes in sequence. The two forms can reinforce each other: a sustained emotional state lowers the threshold for intrusive thoughts; intrusive thoughts intensify emotional distress.

What is important to understand is that neither form validates nor invalidates the other. The person who feels overwhelmed but does not think about suicide is not suffering less than the person who does. They are suffering differently. And different suffering requires a different understanding.

The Danger of Misreading

The failure to understand these distinctions produces a particular kind of damage.

When we calibrate our concern only to visible, cognitive signals — *Is there a plan? Are there thoughts?* — We risk missing the person who is functioning externally while drowning internally. We risk concluding that someone is *fine* because they are present, composed, and free of articulable ideation. We risk confusing the absence of clear thoughts with the absence of crisis.

And we risk something more insidious still: we risk teaching the person in distress that their experience does not qualify. That what they are carrying is not serious enough to name, not clear enough to bring to anyone, not real enough to warrant help.

That lesson, quietly absorbed, tends to extend the suffering.

Function and Meaning Are Not the Same Thing

Modern approaches to mental health recovery are largely organised around function — returning to work, resuming relationships, restoring productivity. These are not trivial goals. For many people, restored function is a genuine measure of progress.

But function answers a different question from the one this book is investigating.

Function asks: *Can I go on?*

The question underneath despair — the question that does not disappear when function is restored — is: *Why should I go on?*

A person can be mentally active, socially engaged, and professionally effective while quietly carrying that second question. The first question is addressed by treatment, routine, and time. The second question requires something deeper — something that gives the continuation of life a reason beyond the mere absence of collapse.

This is where clinical intervention, valuable as it is, reaches its limits. And where the search this book is undertaking begins in earnest.

By now, one thing should be clear: despair is not a uniform experience. It is emotional, cognitive, sometimes both, frequently hidden, and persistently misunderstood. Which means the search for an anchor must be broad enough to hold all of it — not only the suffering that can be named, but the suffering that can only be felt.

Because, regardless of how despair presents, the underlying question remains the same.

Why stay alive?

Naming the experience has not answered it. It has only clarified what we are actually asking. And to pursue the answer, we must begin where most people begin when they are struggling — with the things modern life has told them should be enough.

CHAPTER 3 — *The Question Most People Avoid*

There are questions people are taught not to ask. Not because they are meaningless, but because they are too close to something uncomfortable. The question at the centre of this book is one of them.

It does not usually appear in polite conversation. It is rarely explored openly. And when it does surface, it is often quickly softened, redirected, or shut down — replaced with something safer, something that assumes the answer before the question has been properly heard.

Why stay alive?

Most people do not ask it out loud, even when they feel it. Because the moment the question is spoken, something shifts. It is no longer assumed that life is self-justifying. It is no longer taken for granted that continuing is obvious. The question exposes something many people live with but rarely confront: that the reason for continuing to live is not always clear.

So instead, the question is managed. Replaced with alternatives that feel more navigable: *How do I improve my life? How do I become happier? How do I cope better?* All important questions. But none of them reaches the same depth — because all of them assume, without examination, that life is already justified. There are questions about the quality of a journey whose continuation has already been decided. The deeper question asks whether the journey is worth making at all.

In my own experience, this question did not arrive dramatically.

It did not come as a philosophical curiosity or a moment of crisis with a clear before-and-after. It emerged more quietly — almost indirectly, not as a sentence, but as a tension. There were stretches when everything continued as normal on the surface: work was done, conversations happened, responsibilities were met. And yet underneath, something felt unresolved. A kind of internal dissonance

— as though the act of continuing did not quite match the reason for continuing.

It is difficult to explain this without reducing it to something simpler than it is. Because the question did not always present itself clearly as *Why stay alive?* Sometimes it felt like a sense of disconnection. Sometimes as a sense that effort and meaning were no longer aligned. Sometimes as a quiet but persistent awareness that the usual reasons people rely on no longer carried the same weight they once had.

Over time, that tension takes shape. It becomes more defined. More difficult to ignore. Until eventually, whether spoken or not, the question is there.

Why continue living?

At this point, a set of familiar responses tends to arrive. They are well-intentioned, often repeated, and not entirely wrong: *Life is a gift. Things will get better. Focus on the positive. You have so much to be grateful for.* These responses are not without value. But they consistently fail to address the question as it is actually being asked.

Because there is a difference — a crucial one — between *life containing good things,* and *life is meaningful enough to continue.* The first can be entirely true, and the second can remain entirely unanswered. A person can look at their life, register its genuine contents — relationships, moments of pleasure, periods of achievement — and still find that none of it quite addresses the pressure underneath. The question is not whether good things exist. It is whether those things constitute sufficient grounds for continuing when the weight of life itself becomes difficult to carry.

This distinction is not philosophical hair-splitting. It is the exact gap between what most conventional support offers and what despair is actually asking for.

The philosopher Albert Camus opened his essay *The Myth of Sisyphus* with the assertion that there is only one truly serious philosophical question, and that is suicide — whether life is worth living. [1] He was not being provocative for its own sake. He was naming something that most formal philosophy had conspicuously avoided: that the decision to continue living is not a given, and that a life examined honestly will eventually have to address its own justification.

What Camus identified at the philosophical level, many people encounter at the experiential level — not in seminars or essays, but in the accumulated weight of ordinary days that have somehow lost their coherence.

The things people typically rely on for that justification are real and significant. But they tend to answer different questions from the one despair is posing. Achievement answers *what can I accomplish?* Pleasure answers *what can I enjoy?* Relationships answer *the question, 'Who can I connect with?'* Stability answers *how I can function?* These are not trivial answers. When life is intact, they can feel entirely sufficient — sufficient enough that the deeper question never fully forms. [2]

But they are answers to questions about the contents of life, not to the question of life's continuation. And when life implodes — when assumptions break, when effort no longer produces expected outcomes, when emotional weight becomes difficult to carry — their limits become visible. The question they cannot answer surfaces, and it does not easily go away.

Many people go through life without ever allowing this question to form fully. Not because they have resolved it, but because they have never had to confront it directly. Life provides enough momentum, enough structure, enough distraction to keep the question at a manageable distance. The machinery of daily existence — routine, obligation, small pleasures, the pressure of other people's expectations — carries them forward without requiring a clear account of why.

But when that machinery stops, or slows, or breaks — the question that was always underneath becomes the only question.

And it cannot be answered abstractly. A theoretical response is not enough. A general statement about the value of life is not enough. A borrowed belief, accepted without examination, is not enough. Because the question is not being asked in abstraction, it is being asked from within lived experience, under real weight, in real time. Which means that whatever answer exists — if one exists — must be capable of meeting that experience where it actually is.

It must hold under emotional weight. Under uncertainty. Under disappointment. Under sustained difficulty. Under the specific pressure of a life that has not gone as expected, or has gone exactly as expected and still arrived somewhere that feels unlivable.

Otherwise, it is not an anchor. It is only an idea. And ideas, however elegant, do not hold when the ground gives way.

From this point forward, the approach must change.

We will not assume that life is inherently meaningful. We will not assume that the answers people commonly reach for are sufficient. We will not assume that the first explanation offered is the correct one, or that any explanation is correct until it has been tested against the full weight of what it is being asked to bear.

Instead, we will begin examining where people actually look when they need a reason to continue living. The places modern life directs them. The promises those places make. And whether, under genuine pressure, those promises hold.

The question has been allowed to stand. The investigation now has its terms. What remains is to follow it — carefully, honestly, and without deciding in advance where it leads.

CHAPTER 4 — *When the Question Turns Toward Exit*

There are moments when the question changes.

Not in wording alone. In direction.

Up to a point, the question has been *Why stay alive?* But under sustained pressure — when the weight does not lift, when relief does not arrive, when meaning does not reassemble — the question can begin to turn. Not loudly. Not always clearly. But decisively.

Do I have to?

It is at this point that the landscape shifts. Because the question is no longer only about meaning, it begins to include the possibility of ending the search altogether.

In the world outside this page, that possibility has names. Some call it suicide. Others encounter it through discussions of assisted dying, medical aid in dying, or euthanasia — particularly in contexts where suffering is prolonged, and relief appears uncertain or impossible. These are not abstract ideas. They are real considerations that people arrive at under certain conditions. Not always suddenly. More often, gradually — through accumulation.

The distinction between these contexts matters, and this book is not equipped to resolve the ethical debates that surround assisted dying in terminal illness. What it can observe is that the underlying psychological movement — the turn toward exit as a response to intolerable experience — shares certain characteristics across both. And it is that movement, and what drives it, that this chapter is concerned with.

The movement toward exit rarely begins as a fully formed decision. It begins earlier. As pressure. As fatigue. A growing sense that continuing may require more than what one currently has. In that state, the mind does something both simple and profound — it begins to look for a way out. Not necessarily out of a desire for death, but out of a need for relief.

Psychological work in this area has consistently found that what is commonly described as suicidal desire is more accurately understood as a response to intolerable psychological pain — what Shneidman called *psychache* — rather than a pure wish to cease existing. [1] The target is not non-existence. The target is the end of an experience that has become unbearable: the persistence, the weight, the sense of being enclosed in something that does not resolve.

This distinction changes what is actually being sought. And it changes what the search for an anchor must be able to offer. If what is being sought is not death but relief — not ending but escape from a specific unbearable state — then the question becomes more precise: is ending life the only form that relief can take? Or is it the most immediate conclusion the mind reaches when it cannot yet see another?

That is not a rhetorical question. It is this book's central investigative question, and it will not be answered until the search is complete.

When that sense of an intolerable experience persists without interruption, the idea of stopping it entirely can begin to seem not extreme but conceivable. And with that shift comes something else — a sense of control.

In a situation where much feels unmanageable — where meaning is unclear, where emotional states are persistent, where circumstances do not yield — the idea that one could choose an endpoint carries a particular psychological weight. Thomas Joiner's research into the interpersonal conditions of suicide identified perceived burdensomeness and thwarted belonging as key drivers, but also noted that the acquisition of capability — the sense that one could act — plays a significant role in how individuals relate to overwhelming internal states. [2] In that sense, the idea of exit is not only about ending. It is also about the recovery of agency over an experience that feels otherwise entirely dictated.

This does not exist a solution. It makes it comprehensible. And comprehension — without endorsement, without dismissal — is what an honest investigation requires.

There is a more personal account that belongs here, and it requires being named directly.

At a particular point in my life, during a period when financial pressure on my family in the United Kingdom had become acute, I found myself scouting for Phase 1 clinical trials in London. First-in-Human studies. The kind that introduces untested compounds into a healthy human body to establish toxicity thresholds, adverse reaction profiles, and survivable dosage ranges. Participants in such studies sign consent forms that itemise, with clinical precision, the risks they are accepting.

The official language calls it volunteering. I called it survival—specifically, survival for others. Money generated by placing my body in documented risk would support my family's upkeep. That was the calculus. And within that calculus, the risk to myself was not the troubling part. It was, in a specific and now recognisable way, the point.

What I did not have language for at the time — and what Joiner's framework, encountered years later, would provide — is the precise name for what I was doing. Perceived burdensomeness. An internal accounting that concludes: my existence in life costs more than it contributes to life, and therefore the responsible act is to convert my existence into something useful, even at personal risk. The logic is not irrational. Under sustained pressure, with diminished resources and a family depending on continuation, it approaches something that feels almost reasonable, which is exactly what makes it worth examining carefully. [3]

Because the question underneath the First-in-Human calculation was not, on its surface, *do I want to die?* It was something closer to: *what is my life actually for, and is the risk of it an acceptable currency?* That is not suicidal ideation as it is clinically defined. It is something adjacent — and in some ways more difficult to detect, because it wears the clothing of responsibility rather than despair. It arrived not dramatically but practically. Not as a wish but as a solution. As a way of being useful in a situation where simply being alive did not feel like 'usefulness' enough.

Things are, I should say, very different today. But not because the question resolved itself through better circumstances. But because something else reached it first.

What that something is belongs to a later chapter. The investigation is not there yet.

There is another layer to this that is rarely discussed. Silence.

People do not always speak about these considerations. Not because they are insignificant — frequently they are the most significant thing happening in a person's interior life — but because they are difficult to express without being misunderstood.

There is a gap between what is felt and what can be said.

To say *"I am thinking about ending my life"* is not always to say *"I want to die."* Sometimes it is closer to saying, *"I cannot continue like this."* But those two statements are routinely heard as the same. The response they generate — alarm, intervention, assessment — is calibrated to the first statement, not the second. And so, the person who meant the second learns to say neither. The experience remains internal. A private negotiation between continuing and not continuing, conducted without a witness, without language, and without the possibility of being accurately heard.

This silence is not stubbornness or concealment. It is a rational response to the experience of being misunderstood when the stakes are highest. And it means that many people engaged in this negotiation are doing so entirely alone — not because no one is present, but because no available language captures what they actually mean.

That gap is part of what this book is attempting to address.

The investigation must remain steady here. Because dismissing the movement toward exit does not remove it. And reducing it to a single explanation — crisis, illness, irrationality — does not do justice to its complexity or to the people who experience it.

What can be said, carefully and without minimising the intensity of what is being felt, is this: if the impulse toward exit is rooted primarily in the need to end an unbearable experience rather than in a pure desire for death, then the search for an anchor is not yet complete. There may be something — not a distraction, not a temporary relief, but something structurally capable of meeting the experience — that the investigation has not yet reached.

That possibility keeps the question open. Not:

Should life end?

But:

What is it about life, as it is currently experienced, that feels impossible to continue? And is there anything that can meet that experience without requiring its removal?

These are the questions that drive what follows.

The next section of the search turns toward the places people most commonly look when they need a reason to continue living. Not toward ending the experience, but toward filling it — giving it purpose, productivity, forward motion. These are the anchors modern life most readily offers.

They deserve to be examined honestly. Which means examining not only what they provide, but what they cannot — and whether, under the specific weight of a life that has turned toward exit, they have ever been enough.

CHAPTER 5 — *What Pleasure Promises*

Sofia had, by most measures, built a good life.

The job was demanding but rewarding. The flat was hers. Friday evenings meant a particular restaurant, a particular table, a glass of something cold, and the specific relief of a week finished. Weekends had their own rhythm — markets in the morning, films in the afternoon, the low hum of a social life that was neither too full nor too empty. She had learned, over the years, what made her feel better and had arranged her life accordingly. When things were difficult, she knew what to reach for. When things were good, she knew how to inhabit them.

From the outside, this looked like contentment. From the inside, it felt like competence, which she had always considered close enough.

Then, without a single dramatic event, the rhythm stopped working.

Nothing was removed. The restaurant was still there. The Fridays still arrived. The flat was still hers. But somewhere in the texture of it, something had changed. The relief at the end of the week was shorter than it used to be. The pleasure was still present — she could identify it, name it, point to it — but it no longer seemed to reach anything. It interrupted. Then the weight returned. She found herself, on a Saturday morning, with a coffee and nothing required of her, sitting with a question she had no preparation for.

Is this enough?

She did not know how to answer it. More precisely, she did not know why, with everything in place, it even needed to be asked.

Before the weight arrives — before life implodes and the question becomes unavoidable — most people are living inside an answer they have never had to examine.

Not a philosophical answer. Not considered one. An absorbed one. The kind that does not announce itself because it does not need to — because life, in sufficient quantities, appears to confirm it daily.

The answer is this: that life is justified by how it feels. By the accumulation of moments that make experience worthwhile. Not constant enjoyment — nobody seriously expects that. But enough. Enough relief at the end of a difficult day. Enough pleasure to interrupt discomfort. Enough ease to make continuing feel, if not inspired, then at least reasonable.

This assumption is so widely shared that most people have never identified it as an assumption. It operates silently, beneath the surface of ordinary decisions: looking forward to something, planning a break, turning instinctively toward whatever makes experience lighter. These are not trivial movements. For many people, they are precisely what makes life feel manageable. Sometimes they are what make life feel worth continuing. And when they are present in the right proportion, they create a rhythm — effort followed by relief, strain interrupted by ease — within which the deeper question rarely surfaces, because the experience itself appears to answer it.

But that answer depends on something that is not always stable. It depends on the continued availability of those moments. Or at minimum, on the belief that they will return.

There is a specific kind of difficulty that arrives not when pleasure disappears entirely, but when it loses its reach.

It is difficult to describe precisely because the change is not always visible from the outside. The same experiences are still available. The same opportunities remain. And yet something has shifted — not the presence of pleasure, but its capacity to carry weight. A moment can still be pleasant. Still objectively good. Still, something that, at another time, might have felt sufficient. But now it does not seem to answer anything. It interrupts the weight, briefly. Then the weight returns, unchanged.

This experience has a psychological name. Hedonic adaptation —
sometimes called the hedonic treadmill — describes the documented
tendency of human beings to return to a relatively stable emotional
baseline after both positive and negative events. [1] Pleasurable
experience is, by its nature, transient and adaptive: it diminishes in
impact as it is repeated, and its capacity to sustain long-term
satisfaction is limited. Enjoyment does not accumulate into something
stable. It resets.

This is not a character flaw in the people who experience it. It is a
feature of how pleasure operates, which means that a life built primarily
on the foundation of positive experience is built on something that
moves — something that cannot, by its nature, hold still.

What makes this particularly relevant to the question this book is
pursuing is the specific way pleasure fails under pressure.

When life is intact — when energy is available, when interest is present,
when circumstances permit — pleasure functions adequately as a
working answer to the question of continuation. It is only when those
conditions change that the limitation becomes visible, when energy
drops, when interest fades. When even things that once felt engaging
begin to feel distant. At that point, the assumption that life is justified
by enjoyment becomes harder to sustain — not because enjoyment has
no value, but because it is no longer present in a way that can bear
weight.

And this reveals something important that rarely gets named clearly.

There is a difference between what makes life feel good and what
makes life worth continuing.

These are routinely treated as the same thing. They are not.
Psychological research drawing on the distinction between hedonic and
eudaimonic well-being has consistently found that a life rich in
pleasurable experience may still feel empty if it lacks a sense of purpose
or coherence — that the felt quality of life and its perceived meaning
operate through different mechanisms and respond to different

conditions. [2] Pleasure addresses the first. It has limited purchase on the second.

For some people, when pleasure begins to lose its reach, the response is to intensify the pursuit. To seek more different experiences, stronger stimulation, and more frequent interruption of discomfort. This can provide relief, and relief isn't nothing. But it introduces a dependency that alters the relationship between enjoyment and meaning, often deepening rather than resolving the underlying problem.

Because at a certain point, pleasure stops being something that enriches life and becomes something that must be maintained in order for life to feel bearable. It stops being an accompaniment to living and becomes the condition under which living is possible. And when that shift occurs — when the question of *why continue?* can only be answered by pointing to the next available pleasure — two things follow.

The first is that the answer becomes fragile. Because pleasure cannot always be controlled. Circumstances change. Health changes. Access changes. The things that once provided sufficient interruption become unavailable or insufficient. And when they do, the question returns — not abstractly, but directly, and with more force than before, because the mechanism that was managing it has failed.

The second is that the answer has quietly changed character. It is no longer a reason for living. It is a condition for tolerating it. And tolerating life is not the same as having a reason to continue it.

This is where pleasure reveals its precise limitation as an anchor.

It can soften experience. It cannot explain it. It can relieve. It cannot justify. And if the question is *why stay alive when life implodes* — when experience is not good, when enjoyment is not available, when the rhythm of effort and relief has broken down — then an answer built on pleasure has nothing left to offer at exactly the moment it is most needed.

That is not a dismissal of pleasure's value. It is an accurate account of its reach. Pleasure belongs in life. It is not strong enough to be the reason for one.

Which means the search must continue. Because if enjoyment cannot carry the full weight of the question, then whatever can must be something other than — or something deeper than — how life feels.

The next place many people look is not inward at experience, but outward at output. Not what life feels like, but what it produces. Not pleasure, but achievement — and what it can and cannot hold.

CHAPTER 6 — *What Achievement Promises*

Dani had spent twenty-two years building toward something, and by any reasonable measure, he had reached it.

The title was senior. The salary reflected it. The office had a view he had once, in a different decade, pointed at from street level and told himself about attaining— not as fantasy, but as instruction. He had been the person others called when decisions needed to be made. His name carried weight in the rooms that mattered. His children knew what he did and were proud of it in the particular way children are proud when the world confirms what they already believed about a parent.

And then, at fifty-two, on an otherwise ordinary Tuesday morning, he sat at the desk he had worked toward for two decades and noticed something he could not immediately name.

Not dissatisfaction. Not burnout. Something quieter and more disorienting than either. A sense that the thing he had arrived at was not quite an answer. That the achievement — real, earned, undeniable — did not seem to resolve the question he had apparently been carrying beneath the ambition all along. He had assumed that reaching this point would settle something. It had not. It had simply made the question more visible.

He did not tell anyone. No language for it did not sound ungrateful.

There is another way people attempt to answer the question of why to continue living, not through what life feels like, but through what life produces.

If pleasure asks, *does life feel good enough to continue living?* — Achievement asks something different. *Can life be made meaningful by what it accomplishes?* This is a subtle but significant shift. It shifts the centre of gravity from experience to output. Life may not always feel good. But perhaps it can still be justified if it is useful. If it produces something. If it amounts to something.

This idea runs deeper than pleasure, and it arrives earlier. It appears in how people are measured from childhood onward — how effort is rewarded, how identity begins to form around what one does rather than who one is. A person studies, works, builds, strives — not only to survive, but to become something. And in that process, a connection forms, rarely announced but persistently reinforced: *I matter because I achieve.*

The pattern is not limited to any particular pathway. It operates identically whether the route is corporate, academic, political, entrepreneurial, or — and this is worth stating plainly for this book's global reach — even in structures that exist entirely outside formal or licit systems. The logic of *control, influence, and impact* as life-justification does not require a salary or a title. It requires only the belief that producing something makes one's existence defensible. The pathway differs. The underlying structure is the same.

Achievement offers something pleasure cannot. It accumulates. Effort builds into something visible. Progress can be tracked. Outcomes can be pointed to. There is a sense of direction — and direction, it turns out, can create meaning where experience alone does not. Psychological research on goal-directed behaviour has consistently found that a sense of accomplishment contributes significantly to perceived purpose and life satisfaction. [1] The promise, in other words, is not empty.

Achievement can organise a life. It can structure time. It can provide reasons to continue living and, in many cases, override difficulty. A person may endure what they do not enjoy because they believe it leads somewhere. That belief is not irrational. For much of life, it is accurate.

But it introduces a dependency. Meaning becomes tied to outcome. The outcome is not always within one's control.

The most instructive account of this dependency comes not from psychology but from literature — and from the life of one of its greatest practitioners.

In 1882, at the height of his fame — *War and Peace* and *Anna Karenina* already written, his reputation established across Europe, his estate secure, his family present — Leo Tolstoy found himself unable to answer a single question: *why not simply end it?* He documented this crisis in *A Confession*, writing with uncomfortable directness that he had to remove ropes from his rooms and stop carrying a gun while hunting because he did not trust himself with the means of exit. He had achieved more than almost any writer of his century. He had produced work that would outlast most of civilisation. And it answered nothing.

"My life had come to a standstill," he wrote. "I could breathe, eat, drink, and sleep, and I could not help doing these things; but there was no life, for there were no wishes the fulfilment of which I could find reasonable." [2]

Tolstoy was not suffering from failure. He was suffering from the specific revelation that success — at its most complete — does not contain within itself the answer to why one should continue living. The achievement had been real. The question had not been about achievement.

This is where the limitation of achievement becomes most evident.

There are moments when effort does not produce what was expected. When progress stalls, when recognition does not come, or when what is achieved does not carry the weight it was assumed to. In those moments, the dependency becomes visible. But the more disorienting discovery — the one Tolstoy documented and the man at the desk experienced — is that achievement can *complete* and still leave the question unanswered. That success is not the same as resolution.

One response to this is to pursue more achievements. At a higher level, on a greater scale, with broader influence. And this can work, for a time. But it deepens rather than resolves the underlying condition. Because meaning has now become something that must be continually produced. Achievement is no longer simply something one does. It becomes something one must continue doing in order to remain justified.

At a personal level, this becomes internalised in a way that is rarely examined because it is rarely spoken about. A person begins to measure themselves not by visible success but by their simple ability to function — to show up, to perform, to contribute, to be useful. And the equation becomes quieter, but no less powerful.

Am I enough if I stop doing?

This question is almost never asked directly. But it is lived in the anxiety that surrounds rest, in the guilt that accompanies illness, in the specific dread of a day with nothing required of it. The person who cannot answer yes to that question is not lazy or ungrateful. They have built their justification for existing on a foundation that requires constant maintenance. And foundations that require constant maintenance are not foundations. They are performances.

When life disrupts the continuity of achievement — through loss, illness, unexpected change, or events that cannot be resolved through effort — the question returns with a precision that earlier stages of the search lacked.

If I cannot achieve in the way I once did — if I cannot produce in the way I expected — what remains?

This is the standard the anchor must meet. Not only when progress is possible, but when it is not. Not only when effort yields results, but when it does not. Not only at fifty-two with a view and a title, but at fifty-two with neither — or at thirty-five, or at seventy, in whatever condition life has arrived at by then.

Achievement can organise a life. It can direct, structure, and in many cases sustain it. But it cannot answer the question of why that life should continue when organisation, direction, and structure are no longer available. Its answer is conditional on the continuation of the very conditions whose disruption generated the question in the first place.

Like pleasure, achievement belongs in life. However, it is not strong enough to be the reason for life.

Which means the search must go deeper — past what life feels like, past what life produces, toward something that depends on neither. Most people, when these two anchors fail, do not immediately look inward. They look sideways. Toward the people around them. Toward what it means to be known, needed, and not alone.

Whether that can hold is what the search must now examine.

CHAPTER 7 — *What Relationships Promise*

They had been friends for eleven years. Not the convenient kind — the kind forged in proximity and maintained by habit — but the deliberate kind, built across distance, sustained through effort, tested by the specific events that reveal whether a person will stay.

She had stayed through the year Marcus lost his job and could not explain why it mattered as much as it did. Through the period after his father died, he became someone he himself did not recognise. Through the stretches when he offered nothing back and she asked nothing in return, simply maintaining the frequency of contact until he could re-enter it.

Marcus did not have many relationships like this. He was not sure anyone did. But he had this one — and on the days when the weight of simply continuing felt like more than he had available, the knowledge that she existed, that she would answer, that somewhere in the world was a person who held an accurate account of who he was, was the thing that most reliably interrupted the descent.

He did not analyse this. It simply worked. The way certain things work before you need to understand them.

The question was whether it would always work.

It is often said — quietly, sometimes with conviction, sometimes simply as the thing one says when no other answer is available — that what makes life worth continuing is not what one achieves or what one experiences, but who one has. Not in theory. In presence. A voice that answers. A person who notices. A relationship that does not require explanation.

For many people, this is not an abstraction. It is the specific thing that has carried them through periods when nothing else could. A conversation that interrupted a downward spiral. A message that arrived at the right moment. A presence that made something heavy feel, if not lighter, then at least not solitary.

There is a reason this appears so consistently across human experience. Psychological and developmental research has established that connection — particularly stable, trusting attachment — plays a central role in emotional regulation, resilience, and the basic capacity to continue functioning under pressure. [1] The promise is not imagined. In some cases, it is not even sufficient. For some people, in some conditions, the relational anchor holds completely. The knowledge that someone would notice, that someone would be affected, that someone somewhere cares — this is enough. Not as philosophy. As a fact.

This makes relationships the most compelling answer the investigation has yet encountered. It is worth sitting with that before examining the limits.

But there is a specific kind of difficulty that exists within even the most genuine connection. It is not a failure of the relationship. It is a feature of the distance between one person's interior experience and another person's access to it.

A person can listen without being able to feel exactly what is being felt. A person can care without being able to carry what is being carried. The most attentive, most committed, most present relationship still operates across a gap — the irreducible distance between one person's interior and another's.

In my own experience, this gap was one of the most disorienting aspects of the struggle. The clinical world had categories that did not quite fit. The faith world had answers that did not quite reach. The people closest to me were present and genuine — and still, what I was experiencing could not be fully transferred. Not because they were unwilling. Because the experience itself resisted the available language. [2] That resistance is not an indictment of the relationships. It is a description of a specific limit that even the best relationships carry.

Research into loneliness has increasingly clarified that it is not primarily social isolation that damages well-being, but the perceived gap between one's internal experience and the degree to which it is understood or shared by others. [3] A person can be surrounded by people who genuinely care and still experience a form of solitude that the relationships cannot dissolve — not because the relationships have failed, but because what is being carried inside exceeds what any relationship can fully receive.

C.S. Lewis spent much of his adult life as a confirmed bachelor, intellectually brilliant, relationally guarded, constructing elaborate philosophical defences of the faith he had come to as an adult. At fifty-eight, he married Joy Davidman — a relationship that by his own account transformed his understanding of what connection could be. Four years later, she died of cancer. He documented what followed in *A Grief Observed*, a journal he kept in the immediate aftermath — writing with an honesty that startled readers who had expected the theologian's composure.

What he described was not simply grief. It was the specific experience of having built an anchor and having it physically removed. *"Her absence is like the sky,"* he wrote, *"spread over everything."* The relationship had been real, had been the most sustaining thing in his life, had functioned as precisely the kind of anchor this chapter is examining. And then it was gone — not because it had been insufficient, but because it had been finite. Because relationships, however profound, exist in time. [4]

This is one dimension of the limit. But there is another, less often named, that operates not through loss but through inversion.

Under sustained internal pressure — the kind that does not resolve quickly, that persists across weeks and months, that continues beneath the surface of a life that is otherwise functioning — a specific shift can occur in how relationships are experienced. The person who is struggling begins to think not only about what they receive from the relationships around them, but about what they bring into them.

Am I adding weight? Am I becoming difficult to hold? Am I giving more strain than support?

These questions do not always reflect reality. But they feel real. And when they do, something significant changes. The relationship that was functioning as an anchor begins to feel like a responsibility — something that must be managed carefully, protected from the full weight of what one is carrying, shielded from the honest account of how things actually are. The connection remains. But its function has inverted.

Psychological research into suicidal crisis has identified perceived burdensomeness — the belief that one's existence constitutes a net cost to those whom one loves — as one of the most consistent drivers of suicidal ideation, precisely because it takes the relational anchor and converts it into the relational argument for exit. [5] The very people who are supposed to be reasons to continue living become, in the distorted accounting of sustained distress, reasons to expire.

This is not a failure of the relationship. It is a description of what sustained suffering does to the experience of connection. And it means that the relational anchor, even when it is genuine and present and reciprocal, can be turned against itself by the very condition it is being asked to hold.

None of this removes the importance of relationships. They are, across the full arc of human experience, among the most powerful forces available for sustaining life. The investigation is not arguing otherwise.

But it is asking a more precise question — not whether relationships are meaningful, but whether they are *sufficient*. Whether they can carry the full weight of *why continue living* under all conditions. Whether they hold when they are disrupted by loss. Whether they hold when the gap between felt experience and available understanding cannot be bridged. Whether they hold when the very act of receiving support begins to feel like a burden.

The honest answer, across all those conditions, is: not always. Not unconditionally. Not without depending on variables — presence, continuity, mutual availability, the absence of loss — that are not within one's control.

Something that cannot hold under all conditions is not an anchor. It is a support. And supports, however valuable, are not the same as foundations.

Which means the search must continue. Past what life feels like, past what it produces, past who it is lived with — toward something that does not depend on any of these things. Something that could remain even when pleasure is absent, achievement is impossible, and the relationships that sustain us are disrupted, lost, or turned by distress against their own function.

Whether anything answering that description actually exists is the question the investigation has been building toward. It is time to examine more directly where people have historically looked for it.

CHAPTER 8 — *What Identity and Ideology Promise*

Karim had joined the movement at twenty-three, in the particular way people join things when they are young enough to give themselves completely and hungry enough for a framework that makes the world legible.

It had given him everything the previous years had not. Direction. Community. A vocabulary for the things he had always felt but could not previously name. A set of convictions clear enough to act on and large enough to organise a life around. He knew what he stood for. He knew who stood with him. He knew what the struggle was and what his part in it looked like.

For nearly a decade, this was sufficient. More than sufficient. It was the thing that made getting up in the morning feel like it carried a weight beyond the personal. His own difficulties — and there were difficulties, quiet and persistent — were absorbed by the larger narrative. Endurance was not suffering. It was a contribution.

Then, gradually, something began to shift. Not in the movement — in him. Experiences that the framework had no category for. Questions that the ideology could not cleanly resolve. A growing gap between what the system said his life meant and what his life, as he was actually living it, felt like.

He did not leave. Not immediately. He continued to speak the language, to show up, to perform the identity. But the weight it had once carried had changed. He was still who he had said he was. He just was not sure, any longer, what that meant.

There is a point in the search where the question turns inward — not toward what life feels like, not toward what it produces, not even toward who is present within it, but toward something more fundamental.

Who am I? And what do I belong to?

For many people, this becomes the next place where they seek meaning. Not in fluctuating experience. Not in outcomes that depend on circumstance. But in identity, in becoming something that defines life beyond what happens to it.

This shift carries a specific kind of strength, and it is worth understanding why before examining its limits. Identity is not as immediately disrupted as pleasure. It does not depend as directly on external success as achievement. It is not as vulnerable to loss as a relationship. A person may find that enjoyment has faded, that progress has stalled, that the people who once anchored them are no longer present — and still retain a sense of who they are and what they stand for. That continuity can be genuinely sustaining.

Identity can form around many things: profession, culture, background, values, and vocation. Or something more structured — a cause, a movement, a system of thought that says *this is what I stand for, this is what my life is aligned with, this is what gives it direction beyond myself.* Erik Erikson, who gave the modern world the language of identity development, understood it not as a fixed possession but as an ongoing negotiation — a continuous process of integrating who one has been, who one is, and who one is becoming into something coherent enough to act from. [1] When that negotiation succeeds, the result is not just self-knowledge. It is a framework through which life is interpreted. Events are no longer merely random. Struggle becomes part of a story. Difficulty becomes part of something larger. Endurance acquires meaning because it serves something beyond the immediate.

Psychological research in Social Identity Theory has confirmed what lived experience already knows: that a strong sense of group belonging can significantly enhance resilience, particularly when individuals perceive themselves as part of something that extends beyond their immediate circumstances. [2] The promise is genuine. It can organise thought, direct action, provide clarity in times of confusion, and sustain a person through hardships that would otherwise be unendurable.

But something begins to surface under pressure.

Identity is not as fixed as it first appears.

This is not because people are inconsistent or uncommitted. It is because identity — and this is the chapter's central observation — does not exist only inside the person who holds it. It exists, in significant part, in recognition. A person is seen in a certain way, understood within a certain framework, and placed in a certain category by those around them. That external reception reinforces the internal sense of self. When it is present and consistent, identity feels stable. When it is withdrawn, misunderstood, or challenged — when the role changes, when the community disperses, when the recognition is no longer forthcoming — the internal experience of identity can feel less certain than it appeared.

This is not a weakness. It is the structure of how identity operates. But it means that an anchor whose stability depends on external recognition is not entirely within one's control. It is subject to the same category of disruption — circumstantial, relational, contextual — as the previously noted anchors.

And there is a more internal version of the same disruption. A person who has defined themselves by a particular role may find that role changing. A set of convictions held with certainty may, under the accumulated pressure of lived experience, begin to feel less certain. Not because the convictions were necessarily wrong, but because experience has introduced complexity that they do not fully account for. A question forms — quietly, not urgently, but persistently.

Was that who I was? Or who I believed I was?

And if those changes — what remains?

Ideology extends this territory into something more structured: not merely a personal sense of identity, but alignment with a system of thought that provides explanations, priorities, and direction. Used broadly — as it must be used if this book is to reach across cultures and contexts — ideology encompasses political conviction, religious framework, philosophical worldview, ethnic and communal belonging, any organised system through which a person interprets the world and their place within it.

The strength of ideological anchoring is precisely its comprehensiveness. A person does not have to decide everything from first principles. They can step into an existing framework that has already organised the complexity of existence into a structured, actionable framework. This can be profoundly stabilising — particularly for people navigating uncertainty, trauma, or the kind of sustained internal pressure this book is concerned with.

Arthur Koestler spent the most formative decade of his adult life inside one of the twentieth century's most totalising ideological frameworks, finding in it exactly what this chapter describes: coherence, community, direction, and a narrative within which personal suffering acquired collective meaning. In his contribution to *The God That Failed* — a 1949 collection in which six prominent intellectuals documented their disillusionment with communism — he traced the precise moment the framework began to fail. Not through external attack. Through internal contradiction. Through the accumulation of experiences, the system had no category for, until the gap between what the ideology said reality was and what reality was actually producing became too wide to maintain. [3]

"The whole was greater than its parts," he wrote of his time inside the movement — and then, of what happened when the whole began to fracture: a specific kind of disorientation that had no available language because the language itself had been provided by the framework that was dissolving.

The strength of the ideological anchor and the nature of its failure are the same thing. Its comprehensiveness — the fact that it organises everything — means that when it encounters what it cannot organise, the disruption is not localised. It spreads.

The MLK anecdote does something the Koestler account cannot — it shows the identity anchor not merely failing but actively preventing the person it was supposed to sustain from seeking help. In late 1967, Martin Luther King Jr. sat at the dining table of his personal physician,

Dr Arthur Logan, in the presence of his two closest advisers, Stanley Levison and Clarence Jones. Logan told him directly that he was depressed and that he would benefit from specialist psychiatric treatment. King refused.

The refusal was not irrational. It was the identity anchor operating with precise internal logic. King's public standing — his capacity to lead the movement, to be taken seriously by those he was trying to persuade, to maintain the moral authority on which everything depended — was inseparable from the perception of his psychological strength. A psychiatric referral, if it became known, would hand his opponents exactly the instrument they needed to dismiss him. The identity that had given his life its organising framework was, by 1967, actively constraining his access to the care that the framework's strain was generating. [4]

This is the burden-inversion argument in its most precise biographical form. The relationship — in this case, not a personal connection but a public identity — had completely inverted its function. What was supposed to sustain him had become the reason he could not seek sustenance. The ideological anchor, at the point of its most visible strain, was not merely failing to hold. It was holding him in place, preventing anything else from reaching him.

King carried his depression without clinical intervention for the remaining months of his life. He was assassinated on 04th April 1968.

This is where identity and ideology reach their precise limit as anchors. Not because they lack value — they are among the most powerful organising forces available to human beings — but because their stability depends on conditions they cannot fully control.

Identity depends on continuity of role, of recognition, of the internal coherence that experience can disrupt. Ideology depends on the framework's capacity to account for lived reality — and lived reality, particularly at its most extreme, has a way of exceeding any framework's reach.

Can identity answer the question: *why stay alive when who I am feels uncertain?*

Can ideology answer the question: *why continue living when the system I belong to does not fully explain what I am experiencing?*

Under the specific conditions this book is concerned with — sustained emotional weight, the collapse of assumed meaning, the question that will not resolve — the honest answer is: not unconditionally. Not without depending on the very stability they are being asked to provide.

Something remains unresolved. Not abstractly — specifically. The question presses past what identity defines and ideology organises, toward a territory that neither has fully mapped.

The investigation has now examined five anchors. Each has been found genuinely valuable and genuinely insufficient. What emerges from that accumulation is not despair but precision: a clearer picture of what any answer must be capable of doing that none of these has done. It must hold without requiring continuous maintenance. It must remain when recognition is withdrawn. It must account for what frameworks cannot organise. It must reach what relationships cannot transfer.

Whether anything exists that meets all of these conditions is the question that now drives the search into territory that is less familiar, and perhaps more honest, than what has come before.

CHAPTER 9 — *What Control and Regulation Provide*

Nadia had discovered, in the third year of what she had stopped trying to name, that certain things worked.

Not in the sense of solving anything. In the sense of preventing further descent. A walk before the day began — not for pleasure, she had given up expecting that, but for the specific effect of movement on the thing that happened in her chest in the early mornings. A notebook kept by the bed. A breathing pattern she had learned from a physiotherapist who had not asked too many questions and had shown her something that helped. A rigid structure to the first two hours of the day, because structure was the only thing that reliably delayed the onset of the weight gain.

None of this was happiness. She was not confused about that. But it was functional — and functional, she had come to understand, isn't nothing. It was, in the specific vocabulary of someone who had spent considerable time closer to the edge than anyone around her knew, the difference between the day beginning and the day not beginning at all.

She had come to rely on these things with a seriousness that surprised her. Not because they answered anything. But because they kept the floor from disappearing.

What she had not yet asked — what she was not yet in a position to ask — was whether keeping the floor from disappearing was the same as having a reason to stand on it.

There are moments when the search narrows. Not because the question has been answered, but because the weight of it becomes too much to carry all at once. In those moments, something more immediate takes priority. Not meaning nor explanation. But stability. The need to steady what feels unsteady, to quiet what feels overwhelming, to regain — even briefly — a sense that things are not completely out of control.

This is where a different kind of response begins to take shape. A person does not begin by asking why. They begin by doing what helps. They return to small structures. They move their body. They regulate their breathing. They focus on something immediate and manageable. They create order where they can — not because it answers anything, but because it prevents everything from slipping further.

These actions can seem simple. Even ordinary. And yet they work. The human nervous system responds to rhythm, movement, and physiological regulation in ways that directly influence emotional states — Stephen Porges's work on the polyvagal system has demonstrated that the body's capacity to restore a sense of safety operates through mechanisms that are largely independent of cognitive reasoning. [1] Which means that regulation can produce genuine relief even when the circumstances generating the distress remain entirely unchanged. The mind becomes less chaotic. The body begins to settle. The intensity reduces.

Because these responses work, they are returned to. Again, and again. In time, they begin to feel reliable — not in the sense of solving everything, but in the sense of keeping things from becoming unmanageable. And that reliability, when everything else has felt unreliable, can begin to feel like something more than a coping strategy. It can begin to feel like ground.

I know this particular experience from the inside.

What the memoir of my own struggle makes clear — and what clinical language has never quite captured adequately — is that the state I have lived with is not primarily cognitive. It does not respond to reasoning in the way that a thought can be challenged or a belief examined. It is, in the terms I have come to use for it, an emotional encasement: a doom-and-gloom pressure that does not argue, does not reason, but presses. [2] Against that kind of pressure, the standard apparatus of mental self-management — willpower, perspective-shifting, positive reframing — has limited reach. Not because the person applying it is doing it wrong. Because the state being addressed is not generated by the cognitive system that those tools are designed to reach.

What regulation offers in those circumstances is something more modest and, in its modesty, more honest: not resolution, but interruption. Not recovery, but the restoration of just enough stability to remain present. The decisions that feel impossible become slightly less impossible. The daily activities that have become uphill tasks become fractionally less steep. The experience does not lift. But it becomes, temporarily, more survivable. [3]

That is not a small thing. Under sustained pressure — the kind that does not resolve quickly, that persists across weeks and months, that continues beneath the surface of a life that is otherwise functioning — the ability to interrupt the intensity, even briefly, is often what makes the continuation of the search possible. Regulation, at its best, is what keeps a person present long enough for something else to reach them.

But here the investigation must be precise about what this means — and what it does not.

Even when the mind is quieter, even when the body is more settled, even when the immediate pressure has reduced, the question remains. Not as intensely. Not as urgently. But unchanged. A person can be calm and still uncertain. They can be stable and still unconvinced. They can function — and still quietly carry the recognition that functioning is not the same as having a reason to continue.

This is not a failure of the regulation. It is a description of its limit. Clinical and existential observation has long distinguished between the relief of symptoms and the generation of meaning. Irvin Yalom, whose work in existential psychotherapy is built on this distinction, has consistently argued that reducing distress does not automatically produce a reason to live, and that the deeper existential question — why continue living? — remains. — belongs to a different order of inquiry from the one that symptom relief addresses. [4] Viktor Frankl, writing from a context in which physical survival was the immediate question, observed the same thing from a different angle: that existential distress arising from the absence of meaning — what he called *noögenic neurosis* — is categorically different from psychological disorder, and requires a categorically different response. [5]

If something helps a person live but does not explain why they should live, it is not, in the fullest sense, an answer. It is a condition for the search to continue. Which is genuinely, critically valuable, but it is not the same as the thing being searched for.

This brings the investigation to a point that cannot be avoided and that the accumulation of the previous chapters has quietly prepared for.

The word *anchor* has carried a certain looseness throughout this search. It has been used to describe what supports, steadies, or sustains. But that is no longer a precise enough definition. Because pleasure supports. Achievement sustains. Relationships steady. Regulation stabilises. And none of them, as the investigation has found, is what it is looking for.

So, the distinction must be made clearly here before the search continues.

Anchor — in the sense this investigation requires — *"is not what stabilises a person. It is what remains when stabilisation is no longer enough. It is not what reduces the weight of life. It is what gives a reason to continue carrying the weight of life. It is not what makes life feel manageable. It is what makes the continuation of living meaningful even when life does not feel that way."*

This is a different standard. A higher one. And it is the standard against which everything that follows must now be measured — because it is the standard that everything examined so far has, in its own specific way, failed to meet.

This finding does not diminish control and regulation. They are, if anything, clarified by it. They are what make it possible to remain present long enough for the search to reach what it is actually looking for. They are not the anchor. They are what keep the boat from sinking while the anchor is still being sought.

The question has not disappeared. It has simply become more precise. And a question that has become more precise has not moved further from its answer. It has moved closer.

The search continues — now with a clearer account of what it needs to find.

CHAPTER 10 — *When Escape Becomes an Anchor*

For Théo, it had started, as these things tend to, with something entirely reasonable.

The evenings had become difficult — not dramatically, not in ways he could easily explain to anyone, but difficult in the specific sense that the hours between finishing work and sleeping had begun to feel like a space he did not know how to occupy. There was nothing wrong with the evenings themselves. There was nothing particularly wrong with anything. But he had noticed, over several months, that he was increasingly unwilling to sit with the experience of them simply.

The screen helped. Not in any complex way — it held his attention. It kept the part of his mind that, left to its own devices, moved toward places he found increasingly uncomfortable, occupied with something that required nothing from him. He was not under any illusion that this was good for him. He noticed that it worked, in the limited but real sense that it got him through the evening without the weight becoming unmanageable.

Then it began to get him through the mornings, too. Him checking his phone before he had fully woken up. The day pre-empted before it had properly begun. Small interruptions were inserted with increasing regularity into whatever stretches of time had previously been unmediated. He would not have called it escape. He would have called it coping. The distinction, he would later understand, was thinner than he had assumed.

What he had not yet examined was the question the coping was answering. Not *what is wrong* — he had stopped asking that. But *what is being avoided, and at what cost?*

There are moments when neither pleasure, nor achievement, nor connection, nor even the steadiness that regulation can provide, is what a person reaches for. Not because those things have no value — but because, at a certain point, they require something that is no longer available. Energy. Clarity. Capacity. When those begin to thin, the search does not always move toward meaning. Sometimes it moves sideways. Toward escape — not as a philosophy or a position, but as a response. A way of stepping out of an experience that has become too heavy to remain inside.

This is not, to be precise, a moral observation. Under pressure, human beings move toward relief. That is not weakness or failure — it is a neurologically coherent response to states that exceed the system's current capacity to process. Bessel van der Kolk's research into trauma and the body has demonstrated that when the nervous system encounters experience it cannot integrate, it activates automatic avoidance responses rather than chosen ones — the system attempting to protect itself from what it cannot yet metabolise. [1] Understanding escape in this light does not endorse it as a long-term strategy. It explains why it is reached for, and why the people who reach for it are not doing something irrational. They are doing something understandable. The investigation must hold that distinction clearly before examining what escape cannot provide.

In small measures, stepping away from what feels overwhelming is not only understandable — it is necessary. The problem is not the impulse. It is what happens when the impulse becomes structural.

For some, escape takes the form of substance — something that alters the intensity of experience at the neurochemical level, providing relief that is immediate, reliable, and progressively demanding of repetition. For others, it is immersion in external stimulation — the endless scroll, the continuous stream, anything that holds attention just long enough to keep everything else at a distance. For others still, it is withdrawal: a reduction in engagement, a narrowing of life to what can be managed without strain. This last form, withdrawal, is the least visible and, in some ways, the most insidious — because it can be mistaken, from the inside and the outside, for nothing more than quiet.

William Styron, whose account of depressive illness in *Darkness Visible* has already appeared in this investigation, documents with uncomfortable precision how alcohol functioned as his primary management tool for decades. He describes it not as addiction in the conventional sense but as a reliable instrument — the thing that softened the weight enough to make the day survivable. For nearly forty years, it worked. Then, at sixty, his body rejected it, and what the alcohol had been managing arrived without its buffer, at full intensity, all at once. The escape had not resolved anything. It had, in Styron's own account, deferred the day of reckoning while quietly removing his capacity to face it. [2]

This is the structural pattern that neuroscientific and behavioural research has documented across multiple forms of escape: repeated reliance creates reinforcing loops in which short-term relief strengthens the impulse to return. At the same time, the underlying conditions remain unchanged, and the tolerance for facing them without the buffer progressively diminishes. [3] What begins as relief becomes a cycle. Not because a person chooses this deliberately, but because it works in the moment, and what works under pressure is quite often returned to.

In my own experiences, sustained emotional weight makes the logic of escape comprehensible from the inside in a way that clinical description alone does not quite capture.

What the memoir of my own struggles documents is not escape in its more visible forms, but the experience that makes any form of it rational. The feelings that characterised the worst periods were not episodic. They were sustained and enduring — not a passing moment or a sporadic incident, but something that stuck, sometimes for long periods, sometimes in intense episodes. [4] A cycle of emotional pain that did not let up. Emptiness, worthlessness, a heaviness that the passing of time did not reliably reduce. Against that kind of sustained pressure — the kind that exceeds the internal regulatory system's capacity to manage continuously — the appeal of anything that interrupts the continuity of the experience is not difficult to understand. The interruption is not the problem. The problem is when interruption becomes the only available relationship with the experience.

Because interruption is not the same as transformation. And what is not transformed remains. [5]

This is the point at which escape reaches its structural limit as an anchor — and it is worth being precise about why, because the limit is not where it is usually assumed to be.

The limit is not primarily that escape is harmful, though some forms of escape are harmful. It is not primarily that it produces dependency, though it can. It is that escape works by creating distance from an experience — and distance, however effective as a short-term response, is the opposite of what an anchor does. An anchor holds a person *within* life. It does not remove them from it. It makes presence possible, even under pressure. Escape does the reverse: it makes absence possible. And a life that can only be endured at a distance is not a life being held. It is a life being avoided.

Over time, that avoidance changes the way a person relates to their own experience. What once felt difficult but approachable now feels impossible to face directly. Tolerance narrows. Capacity reduces. Not because the person has become weaker, but because the muscle of direct engagement has been progressively unused. The experience is no longer being met. It is being bypassed. And what is bypassed does not become easier to face. It becomes more foreign.

At some point — whether gradually or suddenly — the distance closes. The moment returns. And the underlying question returns with it, unchanged, except that the mechanisms that managed it have become less reliable, and the capacity to face it directly has diminished.

This is not a counsel against all forms of escape. It is a precise account of what escape cannot do. It can temporarily reduce the weight of experience. It cannot carry it. It can interrupt the continuity of suffering. It cannot explain why the suffering is worth enduring. It can make the question quieter for a time. It cannot answer it.

Which means that what the investigation is looking for must be something capable of remaining present within the experience — not above it, not outside it, not at a managed distance from it — but inside it. Something that does not require the experience to be absent in order to function. Something that holds not by removing the weight but by providing a reason to carry it.

The search has now exhausted responses that work by relief, output, connection, structure, or distancing. What remains is the territory where people have historically looked not for relief from the question but for an answer to it. Not for ways of managing the experience of living — but for frameworks that attempt to explain what living is for.

That is where the investigation now turns.

CHAPTER 11 — *What Meaning Frameworks Attempt*

Elena had come to Stoicism the way most people do— through a crisis that existing resources could not address.

The therapist had been competent but limited. The medication had levelled something without lifting anything. The relationships in her life were genuine, but they could not reach whatever was happening beneath them. And so, she had begun to read — not looking for comfort, she had given up expecting that, but looking for a framework. Something that could take what was happening and render it, if not bearable, then at least intelligible.

What she found in Marcus Aurelius, Epictetus, and the Stoic tradition they represented was something she had not encountered in the therapeutic language that had surrounded her: a philosophy that did not flinch from difficulty. That acknowledged suffering as a condition of existence rather than a problem to be solved. That offered, in place of false reassurance, a rigorous distinction between what was within her power and what was not — and insisted, quietly but firmly, that the boundary between those two things was the only territory worth inhabiting.

She read obsessively. She took notes. She built, over several months, a mental architecture that genuinely changed how she related to the events of her life. Less reactive. More deliberate. More capable of standing inside difficulty without being undone by it.

It worked. That was the thing she kept returning to, even later, when the limits became apparent. It had genuinely worked. The question that eventually pressed through the architecture was not whether the framework was useful. It was whether it was enough.

Enough for what? Elena was only gradually able to articulate. Not enough to stop the days from feeling, in some fundamental register, unjustified.

There is a point in the search where the question is no longer avoided, managed, or postponed. It is engaged — not emotionally, not reactively, but deliberately. If meaning is not immediately apparent, then perhaps it must be constructed. If life does not explain itself, then perhaps it must be explained.

This is where the investigation turns toward what might be called meaning frameworks: not what stabilises life or distracts from it, but what attempts to interpret it. These frameworks do not begin with relief. They begin with thought. They ask what life is, what suffering is, what is within one's control and what is not — and from those questions, they begin to build something. A way of understanding that is durable enough to live inside.

The investigation examines two primary traditions here. Not because they are the only ones — the Buddhist philosophy of impermanence and the liberation found within it, the Confucian framework of relational meaning, the indigenous wisdom traditions of numerous cultures all address this territory with comparable rigour — but because they represent the two dominant Western approaches to the question and their limits are instructive precisely because their starting assumptions are so different.

The Stoic tradition begins with a simple distinction that is demanding to maintain: there are things within one's control, and there are things outside of one's control. Peace, the Stoics propose, is found not by controlling everything but by correctly identifying which is which, and aligning oneself accordingly. Emotional disturbance, in this view, is not caused directly by events but by the judgments made about them. Revise the judgment — and the disturbance revises.

This is not a shallow idea. It has endured for two millennia because it works, in ways that empirical research has subsequently confirmed: cognitive and behavioural psychology, drawing explicitly on Stoic principles, has demonstrated that interpretive frameworks significantly influence emotional response.[1] Marcus Aurelius, writing his *Meditations* as a private journal never intended for publication — a man governing an empire while managing what his own writing suggests was persistent psychological darkness — is among the most credible historical witnesses to the framework's genuine utility. He did not merely theorise the distinction between what is and is not within one's control. He applied it, daily, under conditions of sustained pressure, and the notebooks he left behind are evidence that it provided something real. [2]

But the investigation must ask the specific question this book is concerned with — not whether the framework reduces unnecessary suffering, but whether it answers the question underneath the suffering.

This is where something precise emerges. The Stoic framework excels at reframing experience — at taking what appears chaotic and rendering it structured, what feels overwhelming and making it understandable, what seems like a catastrophe and placing it within a larger context. But context is not justification. To understand something is not always to accept it. And to accept something is not always to find a reason to continue within it.

A person may, through genuine, disciplined application of Stoic principles, come to accept that certain things are outside their control — including the persistent emotional weight this book has been examining. They may learn to hold that weight without being destroyed by it. But acceptance, by itself, does not answer whether continuing to carry the weight is justified. It describes how to relate to the weight. It does not explain why the weight is worth carrying.

And there is a further limit that becomes apparent under the specific conditions this book is most concerned with. The Stoic framework is a cognitive architecture. It requires mental clarity to construct, mental discipline to maintain, and mental effort to apply.

In my own experience of what I have described as emotional encasement — a state that stems from acute situations and what I believe to be a traumatised subconscious, triggered by overwhelming emotional responses that I cannot always discern or escape [3] — the Stoic distinction between what is and is not within one's control encounters a specific difficulty. The state being addressed is not generated by cognitive judgment. It is not a wrong interpretation of events that a right one can correct. It arrives below the level of thought. And a framework calibrated to address thought has limited reach below it.

This does not invalidate the framework. It locates its boundary.

The existentialist tradition approaches the same territory from the opposite direction. Where Stoicism finds peace in aligning oneself with what is, existentialism begins with the acknowledgement that existence precedes essence — that life does not arrive with meaning already built into it. Meaning is not discovered. It is created. A person does not find a purpose; they choose one. And in choosing it, they become responsible for it.

This carries a specific appeal that the Stoic framework does not. It restores agency in a way that feels more honest about the actual condition of existence. Meaning is no longer something handed down by philosophy or circumstance. It is something made — and the making of it is itself an act of self-authorship that carries genuine power.

Camus, who built his entire philosophical project around exactly this territory, lived the tension between the framework's appeal and its fragility more honestly than almost any other twentieth-century thinker. His private notebooks — published posthumously — reveal a man who was not serenely confident in the philosophy of revolt he had constructed, but who was genuinely wrestling with whether it held. [4] His concept of *the absurd* — the gap between human beings' demand for meaning and the universe's silence in response — names precisely what the self-constructed meaning framework is attempting to bridge. And his proposed response, revolt rather than escape, is the most intellectually honest position available within a framework that does not appeal to any source of meaning outside the self.

But the investigation must press the same question here that it pressed against the Stoic framework. If meaning is entirely self-constructed, what gives it weight beyond the will of the person who constructed it? A person may choose a purpose and commit to it fully. But the question remains: why *that* purpose, and not another? And if the person who chose it changes — through illness, loss, the specific erosion that sustained suffering produces — does the meaning change with them?

What is constructed can be reconstructed. What is chosen can be unchosen. This does not render self-constructed meaning useless. It makes it contingent. And the investigation is looking for something that holds under the conditions that make contingency itself feel unbearable — when the will to maintain the framework weakens, when the clarity required to sustain the construction fades, when the sustained emotional pressure that this book is most concerned with makes the cognitive effort of meaning-maintenance difficult to continue.

This is the limit both frameworks share, despite their very different starting points. They are both primarily cognitive architectures. They organise thought, structure interpretation, and provide frameworks through which experience can be understood and, within limits, managed. And at their best, they do this with genuine rigour and genuine effect.

But they meet the same border. There remains a distance between understanding life — even understanding it well, even understanding it with the disciplined clarity that genuine application of either tradition can produce — and having a reason to continue it. That distance is not always large. But it is real. And for the specific experience this book is investigating — the sustained, non-cognitive emotional weight that does not respond to interpretive reframing — it is wide enough that the frameworks do not fully cross it.

What the investigation has learned from this chapter is precise: meaning frameworks can guide, stabilise thought, and organise experience. They can even, in many cases, carry a person through periods of difficulty that would otherwise be unendurable. But they do this through cognition. And the question underneath the suffering this book is concerned with is not primarily cognitive. It is existential in the fullest sense — a question about whether existence itself is justified — and it presses from below the level that cognitive frameworks are designed to reach.

Something else is needed. Not instead of these frameworks — they are valuable and should not be abandoned. But beneath them. Something that does not depend on the clarity, discipline, and will that frameworks require. Something that can hold when the capacity to hold a framework weakens.

Whether anything answering that description exists in the clinical world — in the specific practices designed not to explain life but to stabilise the mind that is living it — is where the search turns next.

CHAPTER 12 — *Can Stabilising the Mind Give a Reason to Live?*

Samuel had been in therapy for fourteen months before he said the thing he had actually come to say.

Not because he was withholding. Because it took that long to find the language, the earlier sessions had covered the obvious territory — childhood, patterns, relationships, the recurring events that the therapeutic framework could organise into something coherent. And this had been genuinely useful. He was less reactive. More self-aware. Better at identifying the moments before they became unmanageable.

But underneath all of that, intact and unaddressed, was the question that had brought him there in the first place. Not *why am I like this?* Not *how do I function better?* But the one he could not quite say aloud because it felt too large, or too ungrateful, or too much like a failure of everything the therapy had so far achieved.

Why continue living at all?

When he finally said it — in the fourteenth month, on a Tuesday afternoon — the therapist did not flinch. But the response, however skilled, was calibrated to what the therapeutic framework was designed to address. Cognitive patterns. Distorted thinking. The interpretive structures that could be examined and revised.

The problem was that the question was not a distorted thought. It was a genuine question. And he left the session with the same sense he had arrived with — that something real and important had been heard, and not quite reached.

There comes a point in the search where the question is no longer approached alone. Not because it has been resolved, but because it has become too complex, too persistent, or too heavy to navigate without assistance. At that point, many people turn toward something more structured than philosophy, more external than self-regulation, more sustained than any of the frameworks the previous chapters have examined.

Clinical support. A different kind of engagement — one that does not begin by asking what life means, but by asking what is happening within the person experiencing it.

This reframing is important, and it should not be underestimated. The shift from *answering the question* to *understanding the condition* has genuine therapeutic value. Patterns are examined, thoughts observed, emotions named. In some approaches, the focus is on cognition — how thoughts form, repeat, and influence perception. In others, on deeper material: past events, internalised patterns, unresolved tensions that have accumulated beneath the surface of a functioning life. In many cases, there is a biological dimension — the recognition that mood, energy, and perception are shaped not only by thought and experience but by underlying neurochemical processes that respond to pharmacological intervention.

For many people, this combination makes a real and measurable difference. Clinical research has consistently demonstrated that evidence-based therapeutic approaches and, where appropriate, pharmacological treatment can significantly reduce symptoms of depression, anxiety, and related conditions. [1] This is not marginal. In many cases, it is the difference between a life that can be continued and one that cannot. The investigation has no interest in understating that.

But it must be honest about what clinical support is designed to do — and what it is not.

My own engagements with the clinical world span decades. I was formally diagnosed with anxiety and depression a decade ago, and years afterwards diagnosed too with autism of the variant that's without intellectual impairment. However, the struggles preceded the diagnoses by a long stretch — years of experience that the diagnostic categories, when they finally arrived, named without fully explaining. The medications that followed were, in the word I have used for them elsewhere, *subsistent* — maintaining a floor without raising what was below it. The therapy sessions available to me at the time were, and I say this without hostility but with the honesty this book's investigation requires, not well-matched to what I was presenting. Not because the practitioners were incompetent, but because the experience I was bringing — the sustained emotional state that is not primarily cognitive, that does not respond to reframing because it is not generated by cognition — fell outside the operational range of the frameworks being applied. [2]

There is a further dimension to the unavailability of clinical support that this book's investigation must name — one that operates not through clinical mismatch but through identity cost. Martin Luther King Jr.'s refusal of psychiatric referral in 1967, examined in Chapter 8 in the context of identity and ideology, belongs here too, in a different analytical capacity. What those refusal documents are not only the identity anchor's failure but the specific way that public identity can make clinical stabilisation structurally inaccessible to the people who most need it.

King's depression was clinically evident to everyone in that room. The diagnosis was not in question. What was in question was the cost of accepting treatment — the specific, calculated cost to the public identity on which everything else depended. The clinical support was available. The person who needed it could not reach it without risking the very framework that gave his life meaning. [3]

This is not an unusual pattern. It is a documented one. The people whose identities are most publicly constructed — whose worth, in their own accounting and the world's, is most closely tied to perceived strength, clarity, and function — are frequently the people for whom the acknowledgement of clinical need carries the highest cost. This book's investigation names this not to discourage seeking help, but to be honest about why people who most need it sometimes don't seek help. That honesty is part of what responsible engagement with this territory requires.

I want to be careful here. This is not an argument against clinical care. The Author's Note of this book already states plainly that professional support — therapies, clinical interventions, honest conversations with doctors — is not a retreat from the search but often what makes the search survivable. That remains true. What I am describing is something more specific: the experience of bringing a subcognitive emotional state into a cognitively calibrated therapeutic framework and finding that the reach, however skilled and genuine, does not quite extend to where the weight actually lives.

This is not an uncommon experience. It is one that the clinical world is increasingly recognising — that certain forms of sustained emotional distress require therapeutic approaches calibrated to their specific nature, not only to their surface symptoms. The match between experience and framework matters. And when it is not present, the absence is not a failure on the part of the person seeking help. It is a gap in the available provision. [4]

William Styron, whose account of depressive illness has appeared at several points in this book's investigation, is the most precisely documented witness to what clinical stabilisation can and cannot provide. His eventual hospitalisation — which he had resisted and which he describes as a surrender rather than a choice — was, by his own account, what kept him alive. He is categorical on this: without it, he would not have survived the winter. He is equally categorical that what broke the depression was not the clinical environment itself but something that arrived unexpectedly within it — a piece of music drifting from another room, carrying a specific emotional resonance that reached something the clinical apparatus had not been able to reach. The hospitalisation provided the conditions. Something else provided the turning. [5]

That distinction — between the conditions that make survival possible and the thing that makes survival meaningful — is the chapter's central finding. And it is not a criticism of clinical care. It is the most honest account of what clinical care does.

There is another dimension to this that this book's investigation must name, because it is almost absent from the standard narratives around mental health recovery.

As stability increases, awareness can increase alongside it. A person who was previously overwhelmed by the intensity of their internal experience may find, as that intensity reduces, that the question the intensity was obscuring becomes more visible rather than less. Not buried under the weight of acute distress. Standing in the open. Requiring a response to the distress that, paradoxically, had previously been deferred.

This is disorienting, and it is worth saying plainly: it is a recognised clinical phenomenon. The reduction of acute symptoms does not automatically justify continued treatment. It can, and sometimes does, make the absence of that reason more apparent. A person who could previously attribute everything to *this is just how I feel*, finds, in stability, that the feeling has reduced, but the question has not. What remains is not residual illness. It is the original inquiry, stripped of its emotional obscuration, asking to be taken seriously on its own terms.

Even if I am stable, what is this life for?

This is where the investigation reaches a threshold that cannot be deferred further.

Everything examined across the preceding chapters — pleasure, achievement, relationships, identity, control, escape, meaning frameworks, clinical stabilisation — has been found necessary in its proper domain and insufficient in the fullest sense. Not because any of these things lack value. But because none of them, individually or in combination, meets the standard the investigation has now precisely defined: something that holds not by managing the weight of life but by giving a reason to carry it. Something that operates not only when conditions are favourable but also when they are not. Something that reaches below the cognitive level that frameworks require and below the symptomatic level that clinical intervention addresses.

The question is whether anything meeting that description actually exists.

This is the point the investigation has been building toward since the Author's Note. Not a point of conclusion — the investigation has made no conclusions — but a point of honest reckoning. The structures most immediately available to modern human beings have been examined with the seriousness they deserve and found, each in its specific way, to reach a border they cannot cross.

What lies beyond that border is not obvious. It is not contemporary. And it will not be reached by looking forward into newer versions of what has already been examined.

The investigation now turns to look in a direction most modern frameworks have stopped looking. Not toward what has been recently constructed — but toward what has endured. Toward the places human beings have historically reached when every immediate resource has been exhausted, and the question has still not been answered.

Whether those places hold anything real is what the search must now find out.

CHAPTER 13 — *Have We Been Here Before?*

Maya had not expected to find it in a library.

Not a resolution — she had stopped expecting that. But something she had not been able to name until she encountered it unexpectedly in the reading room of a university library on a Thursday afternoon, in a translation of a text written approximately three thousand years ago.

She had been reading, with the unfocused attention of someone going through familiar motions, through a sequence of ancient writings her supervisor had assigned for reasons unrelated to anything she was carrying privately. And then a passage stopped her.

Not because it answered anything. Because it is named something, with a precision she had not encountered in any of the contemporary frameworks she had spent the previous two years inside — the therapy, the self-help literature, the philosophical reading, the conversations with people who cared and could not quite reach what she was describing.

The passage was not optimistic. It did not reassure. It did not offer a way through or a reason to continue. It simply described, with an accuracy that felt almost forensic, the specific quality of the experience she had been unable to articulate to anyone adequately.

She sat with it for a long time. Then she read it again.

What shifted was not the weight. The weight remained. What shifted was the isolation. The sense — which had been, in some ways, the most difficult aspect of the whole experience — that she was carrying something entirely private, something that had no precedent, something that existed outside the range of what had already been seen and named and survived.

Someone had been here before. Someone had found language for it. And had written it down.

That was not an answer. But it was not nothing.

There is a point in the search where the direction changes again. Not because the question has been answered — it has not — but because it has resisted every framework available within the present. It has moved through experience, effort, relationship, thought, and structure. It has been examined through pleasure, achievement, connection, identity, control, escape, constructed meaning, and clinical stabilisation. And still it remains. Not louder. But no less present.

At that point, something begins to suggest itself. Not as a conclusion, not as a clear decision, but as a quiet possibility. That this question may not be new, that what feels intensely personal may not be unique. That if the most immediately available frameworks have reached their borders, the answer — if one exists — may lie in territory that those frameworks have stopped visiting.

This is not a nostalgic turn. It is a logical one.

There is a tendency, particularly in the present, to assume that modern life has produced entirely new forms of difficulty. And in some ways, it has — the pace is different, the pressures are different, the structures are different. But beneath those differences, something more constant emerges when the historical record is honestly examined. Human beings in very different contexts — separated by centuries, continents, and entirely distinct cultural frameworks — have encountered experiences that press in recognisably similar ways. Loss. Uncertainty. Suffering that does not resolve easily. Questions that do not yield to simple answers. And in those conditions, the same kind of question surfaces. Not always in the same words. But recognisably the same in substance.

Why continue living?

The philosophical and literary record across cultures and historical periods reveals a sustained, recurring engagement with exactly this territory — not as an abstract intellectual exercise but as a practical, urgent, personal confrontation with the question of whether existence is justified. [1] This does not mean those who came before resolved the question. It means they encountered it. And in encountering it, they left something behind. Not instructions. Not systems to be adopted wholesale. But records of what it looked like to stand in that space — to remain within the question long enough to say something true about it.

Leo Tolstoy, who has already appeared in this investigation as a witness to the failure of achievement as an anchor, documented something else in *A Confession* that is directly relevant here. Having exhausted the frameworks most immediately available to him — literary achievement, family, reason, and the inherited religious doctrine of his culture — he turned, deliberately and with a scholar's rigour, toward traditions he had previously dismissed. Peasant wisdom. Ancient philosophical texts. Non-Western frameworks. Early Christian writings that predated the institutional forms he had rejected.

What he found was not a ready-made answer. What he found was company. Evidence that the question had been carried before, across different traditions and different centuries, by people who had not found it unanswerable simply because it was difficult. [2] His turn toward the ancient and the historical was not a retreat from the question. It was the recognition that the question deserved older witnesses than the nineteenth century could provide.

That recognition is what this chapter is describing. And Tolstoy is not the only one who has made it.

The philosopher Pierre Hadot, who spent a lifetime studying ancient philosophical traditions, made an observation central to the chapter's argument. Ancient philosophy — Stoic, Epicurean, Platonic, and others — was not primarily a theoretical enterprise. It was a practical response to the question of how to live. [3] The ancient philosophical schools were not producing systems to be studied from a distance. They were producing practices — ways of inhabiting existence — developed in direct response to the same confrontation with suffering, uncertainty, and the question of continuation that this book has been examining. They were, in Hadot's precise formulation, *exercises in how to die and how to live*, which is another way of saying they were taking the question this investigation is pursuing with complete seriousness, and doing so over the course of centuries.

This matters because it changes what the investigation is looking for when it turns toward these traditions. Not doctrine. Not instruction. But witness — the record of what it looked like when serious people, under genuine pressure, took the question all the way to its end and reported back honestly on what they found.

Some of what they found will not hold up under examination. The investigation will not adopt ancient wisdom uncritically — that would be the same failure, in a different direction, as adopting any modern framework without examination. But some of what they found has endured not because it was institutionalised or mandated but because it proved, across repeated testing by different people in different conditions, to be true in some sense that outlasted the specific cultural context in which it was first articulated.

That endurance is itself a form of evidence. Not conclusive. But worth taking seriously.

There is also something specific that the historical record does — something the contemporary frameworks have not been able to do — that this chapter's vignette names without explaining it analytically. It de-isolates.

The experience of recognising that someone else, in another time and under different conditions, has already stood in the same place and used language that reaches the experience — this is not a trivial psychological event. Research into what has been termed *temporal self-expansion* — the capacity to locate one's own experience within a historical continuum — suggests that the sense of isolation that accompanies sustained suffering is significantly affected by whether the sufferer perceives their experience as unique or as part of a larger human pattern. [4] To discover that the question has been asked before does not answer it. But it changes how it is held. The urgency to find an immediate answer softens — not because the need for an answer disappears, but because the search itself begins to feel less like an anomaly and more like a continuation of something already underway.

The question is no longer carried as something entirely private. It becomes situated within a larger human experience. Not diluted by that situating. Held differently within it.

This is where the search moves next, not toward conclusions. But toward the voices that did not avoid the question — that did not rush to resolve it, did not soften it into something more manageable, did not answer it before they had earned the answer. Voices that remained within the question long enough to say something true about it.

Not everything they say will hold. The investigation will test what it finds against the same standard it has applied throughout — can this meet the experience of sustained, non-cognitive emotional weight? Can it hold not only when conditions are favourable but also when they are not? Can it reach below the cognitive level that frameworks require?

Some of what the ancient witnesses offer will not pass that test. But some of it might. And the investigation has not found, in any of the modern frameworks, a sufficient reason to stop looking.

That is enough to continue.

CHAPTER 14 — *The Brutal Honesty of Ancient Wisdom*

Elias had studied literature for six years and considered himself, without particular anxiety, an atheist. The texts he was about to encounter, he had always filed, without much thought, under *religious* — a category that, in his personal taxonomy, meant interesting historically but not seriously relevant to the questions he was actually carrying.

He encountered Ecclesiastes first through a secondary source — Harold Bloom's literary criticism, which approached the text not as scripture but as what Bloom called the most sceptical book in the Western canon. A text that had survived three millennia not because it offered comfort but because it refused to. Bloom's reading was secular, rigorous, and entirely uninterested in its devotional reception. What the text said, Bloom argued, was essentially this: that human striving — for wisdom, for pleasure, for achievement, for legacy — runs consistently into the same border. Not failure. Something more disorienting than failure. The discovery that success does not carry what it was assumed to carry.

He read the original text with Bloom's framing in place. And found that the author of Ecclesiastes — whoever it was, writing in whatever century — had already been to every place the preceding chapters of this investigation had visited. And had said, with an economy that three thousand years had not diminished, what each place contained.

He was not converted to anything. But he was no longer able to file the text under *not seriously relevant.*

After everything that has been tested — everything that has helped and yet not held — attention begins to fall on voices that did not begin with solutions. Voices that did not try to fix the question. Only to speak from within it. They seem distant at first. The language is older. The world they describe is different. And yet the experience is not.

This chapter introduces four ancient texts — not as doctrine or scripture requiring prior faith commitments, but as witnesses. Documents produced by serious people under genuine pressure, in different cultures and centuries, who took this investigation's central question all the way to its end and reported honestly on what they found. They are treated here exactly as every other witness in this investigation has been treated: with the full weight of what they actually say, and without the protection of either devotional reverence or dismissive scepticism.

They have earned their place in this investigation by exactly the quality Chapter 13 identified: they did not avoid the question. And they did not answer it cheaply.

Ecclesiastes — The Limits of Everything

The Book of Ecclesiastes is, by any serious literary assessment, one of the most unsentimental documents in the ancient world. Harold Bloom, approaching it as a literary critic rather than a theologian, described it as *the only book in the Bible that is genuinely and profoundly sceptical* — a text whose primary intellectual operation is the systematic dismantling of the assumptions that human beings use to sustain themselves. [1]

The author — writing under the persona of Qohelet, a reflective observer who has pursued wisdom, pleasure, achievement, and meaning with genuine rigour — concludes that the investigation will recognise immediately. Not that these things have no value. But they do not hold as expected. The Hebrew term the text uses repeatedly — *hevel,* conventionally translated as *vanity* but more precisely rendered as *breath* or *vapour* — names the quality of impermanence that the investigation has been identifying in every anchor examined. Pleasure resets. Achievement requires constant maintenance. Meaning frameworks depend on clarity to sustain them. *Hevel.* Each thing is real. Each thing is temporary. Each thing, held alone, is insufficient.

What is striking is not only the observation. It is the tone in which it is made. There is no bitterness. There is clarity — the specific clarity of a person who has examined the available options without illusion and reported on what the examination found. Ecclesiastes does not resolve the question. It strips it of its false answers. And in doing so, it performs exactly the service the investigation has been performing for fourteen chapters. [2]

Marcus Aurelius, writing his *Meditations* in the second century CE — a Stoic pagan emperor with no relationship to the Ecclesiastes tradition — arrived at almost identical conclusions through an entirely different intellectual route. The convergence is itself significant: that these two witnesses, separated by centuries and cultures and entirely distinct frameworks, identified the same border through the same honest examination. [3]

Job — The Refusal to Pretend

If Ecclesiastes approaches the question from the perspective of the observer, the Book of Job approaches it from inside the experience. A person is not analysing suffering from a distance. He is overtaken by it. Loss without explanation. Pain without proportion. Silence where answers are expected. And the people around him — his friends, his community, the voices that represent the available frameworks of his culture — insist on providing explanations that the text itself refuses to endorse.

Carl Jung, in his late work *Answer to Job* (1952) — approached the text as a psychologist rather than a theologian, and caused significant controversy by doing so — identified what he considered the most important moment in the entire document: not Job's suffering, but Job's refusal to accept the explanations offered for it. The friends' frameworks — suffering as punishment, suffering as test, suffering as something that must have a proportionate cause — are presented by the text with sufficient plausibility that a reader might accept them. And then they are rejected. Not by divine revelation, but by the sheer inadequacy of their reach relative to the experience being described. [4]

What Job's text refuses to do is precisely what this book's investigation has been refusing to do since the Author's Note. It will not answer the question before the investigation has earned the answer. It will not force meaning where none is currently visible. It will not pretend that the available frameworks are sufficient when the experience in front of them exceeds their reach.

The text ends in ways that have troubled commentators for centuries — not with a philosophical resolution but with an encounter that defies easy summary. The investigation will return to that ending. But what matters here is what precedes it: the longest sustained biblical account of a person refusing to accept insufficient answers to a genuine question. That refusal is itself a form of intellectual integrity that this book's investigation recognises.

Psalms — The Permission to Move

The Psalms are not a single voice. There are many voices across many centuries, collected because they were recognised as saying something true about the interior life that more composed literature could not reach. What distinguishes them from almost any other ancient literary collection is their refusal to maintain a consistent position.

C.S. Lewis, in *Reflections on the Psalms* — approaching the texts as a literary scholar before a theologian — noted that what made them extraordinary was precisely their emotional honesty. They do not curate the internal life into something presentable. They move from certainty to questioning, from trust to disorientation, from clarity to confusion, sometimes within the same poem and occasionally within the same verse. [5] Some lines sound like resolution, and lines that sound like complete absence. And both are allowed to stand without the text feeling compelled to reconcile them.

This matters for the investigation because it provides something no other ancient text in this chapter does: permission. Permission for the internal life to be unstable without that instability constituting failure. Permission for the question to return after it appeared to have been settled. Permission for the movement between trust and its absence to be not a weakness but an accurate account of what the experience actually is.

The Psalms do not end in disappearance. They do not resolve everything. But neither do they collapse. They remain — not because everything has been explained, not because everything has been made bearable, but because something is holding that is not immediately named. That unnamed holding is what the investigation must now look at directly.

2 Corinthians 4:8–9 — The Thing That Prevents the Final Word

Pressed on every side, but not crushed. Perplexed, but not driven to despair. Struck down, but not destroyed.

This passage — written by Paul of Tarsus from within documented sustained pressure, not from a position of resolution — is the most precise ancient description of what the investigation has been looking for since Chapter 9 redefined the standard an anchor must meet. Not something that removes difficulty. Something that prevents difficulty from having the final word.

The philosopher Gabriel Marcel distinguished between *optimism* and *hope* in a way that illuminates what this passage is describing. Optimism, Marcel argued, is a disposition toward conditions — it expects them to improve. Hope is something structurally different: it persists not because conditions are expected to improve but because something holds beneath them that conditions cannot reach. [6] The 2 Corinthians passage is not describing optimism. The pressure is still present in every clause. The perplexity is still present. The being struck down is still present. What the passage names is not the removal of these things but the presence of something that prevents them from being final.

Pressed — *but not crushed.* Perplexed — *but not driven to despair.* Struck down — *but not destroyed.*

The repeated structure is not rhetorical decoration. It is the grammatical form of an anchor — something that holds within the experience rather than above it or outside it. The first half of each clause is the full weight of the investigation's question. The second half is the thing the investigation has been looking for.

What that thing is — what provides the *but*, in each clause — the passage does not immediately explain. It simply states that it exists. And states it from within the experience, not from the outside.

In my own experience — the young engineer in Port Harcourt who wished the earth were flat so he could walk until he dropped off the edge, the man who years later found himself in London reading consent forms for First-in-Human trials — this passage describes a quality of experience I recognise without yet being able to account for fully. Something that, across the decades and the weight and the accumulated insufficiency of everything else examined, has prevented the pressure from having the final word. I am not ready to name it yet. The investigation is not there.

But I can say this: it is not any of the things the preceding chapters examined. And it is real.

What these four witnesses share — across their different centuries, cultures, and forms — is the quality Chapter 13 identified as the reason to take them seriously. They did not avoid the question. They did not answer it cheaply. And they arrived, through sustained honest engagement with the full weight of human experience, at the same territory: the possibility that something exists which holds not by removing pressure but by outlasting it.

That possibility is not yet a conclusion. The investigation has made no conclusions. But it is no longer theoretical. It has been named by witnesses from multiple directions, who had no reason to name it unless it was true.

The search is now close enough to the thing it has been looking for that the next step is not to examine any other witnesses.

It is to ask, directly and without deflection, what that thing actually is.

CHAPTER 15 — *The Defiance of Remaining*

Amara had been asked, in the fourteenth month of treatment, what had kept her here. The therapist meant it as an opening—an invitation to identify the positive resources that had sustained her during the period before clinical support arrived.

She sat with the question for longer than she felt comfortable.

The honest answer was not what the question was designed to receive. It was not a relationship, though relationships had been present. It was not a purpose, though she had gone through the motions of purpose. It was not hope in any meaningful sense, because hope had been largely absent for an extended stretch of the period in question.

What had kept her there was closer to something she was reluctant to name because it did not sound like a reason. It sounded like the absence of a reason to leave rather than the presence of a reason to stay. A specific, stubborn, unglamorous refusal. Not to struggle — the struggle had continued. But to concede. To hand over, to whatever was pressing her toward the exit, the satisfaction of her departure.

She was not sure this counted as survival in any form she was prepared to celebrate. But she was, undeniably, still there.

That, she finally said, *is what kept me here.*

Some people remain alive without having found a reason to live. Not because the question has been answered. Not because meaning has been located or an anchor has held in any of the ways the preceding chapters examined. But because something in them has refused to step out. Not clarity. Not resolution. Refusal.

At some point in an honest investigation, this must be said plainly. Not everyone who stays is staying because they have found something worth staying for. Some stay because they have not accepted the alternative. This is not the same thing as an anchor in the fullest sense in which the investigation has been pursuing it. And yet it is real. And reality, however unglamorous, is what the investigation is committed to following.

Albert Camus — who appeared in Chapter 3 as the philosopher who named suicide as the only truly serious question — proposed, as his answer to that question, a position he called revolt. Not faith. Not constructed meaning. Not any of the frameworks the investigation has examined. Revolt: the conscious, defiant, sustained refusal to accept the absurd as the final word. To know that the universe offers no response to the human demand for meaning — and to continue anyway. Not in hope of resolution. In refusal of surrender. [1] Camus was not describing a comfortable position. He was describing the most honest one available to a person who has followed the question all the way to its end and found neither resolution nor sufficient reason to exit. The defiance of remaining.

This is not Camus's complete answer, and the investigation does not adopt it wholesale. But he names something that the chapter's more personal material requires a secular intellectual witness to confirm: that *living against* — in the absence of living for — is a recognisable, philosophically coherent, and historically documented human response to the condition this book is examining.

In my own experience, the question did not always meet an answer. There were long stretches where nothing presented itself as sufficient. No clear reason. No stable ground. No anchor that held in the ways the investigation has examined, one by one, across the preceding chapters. And yet I did not leave. Not because I had resolved the question. But because there were things I could not accept.

One of them was this. I could not bring myself to step out of life and then stand before the God (יהוה) I am one hundred per cent convinced exists, by the route of suicide. This was not, on reflection, straightforwardly fear. It was something more precise: an anxiety to please יהוה optimally, before whom I am acutely aware of the gap between what my Christian life has been and what it should have been. The flaws are real. The incompleteness is real. The distance between

what I believe is required and what I have managed is real. And the
thought of arriving before Him through suicide exit— turning up,
uninvited by that route, with that account of stewardship — was, in the
most unguarded moments, the specific thing that prevented me from
going further than I went. Not peace. Not resolution. A barrier built
from conviction and the specific anxiety of a person who wants, more
than almost anything, to get this right.

That is not a testimony. It is an account of what was actually there.

There was also something else — a different kind of resistance, less
theological and more visceral. The awareness, whether perceived or
entirely real, that there are forces that do not wish me well. Some
human. Some not. And the thought emerged, more than once, with a
clarity that surprised me by its steadiness: would suicide be a
concession? Would it hand over something that should not be handed
over? Would it be, in some sense, a cheap victory for the wrong side?

That question did not resolve anything. But it hardened something. A
refusal — not to struggle, the struggle continued — but to surrender.
And from that refusal, a principle began to take shape. Not formally.
Not philosophically. Practically. Forged from the specific pressure of
carrying this question across decades, and tested, in my own small way,
against others carrying similar weight in the congregations I have
served without remuneration:

*If you cannot find what to live for, find what you can live against. If there is nothing
that draws you forward, identify what you will not fall backwards to.*

This is not a philosophy of flourishing. It is a philosophy of remaining.
And remaining, as the investigation has established, is the necessary
condition for anything else.

Winston Churchill documented his depression — his own term was *the
black dog* — across decades of private correspondence and the accounts
of those closest to him. He did not overcome it. He did not resolve it.
He did not locate, in any documented account, a meaning framework
that answered it. What he brought to it was something temperamentally
closer to the position this chapter is describing: an absolute refusal to

concede to it, or to the external forces whose defeat he had made the organising principle of his public life. [2] His survival was, by his own admission, not primarily motivated by positive vision. It was motivated by defiance. By the specific, obstinate refusal to hand over something he opposed, the victory of his absence.

This is not a model for living. It is a documented instance of remaining — and, as the investigation has found, remaining is not nothing. Psychological research into survival under extreme conditions has consistently identified resistance and refusal — even in the absence of positive meaning — as sustaining forces capable of maintaining the will to continue when other resources have been exhausted.[3] Frankl documented this in the camps: that among the mechanisms of survival, defiance — the refusal to let the situation have the final word — functioned as a form of meaning-making in itself, even before more complete meaning was formed.

But Frankl's own framework ultimately requires meaning to complete the arc of survival. And that is precisely where the investigation must be honest about the limits of the defiance position.

Living against is not the same as living for. It can sustain. It has sustained — this is not theoretical; it is documented here and in the historical record. But it cannot be grounded because resistance requires something to resist. And when that something shifts, weakens, or becomes less immediate, the question it was holding at a distance returns.

A person cannot indefinitely define their existence only by opposition. Not because defiance is insufficient as a survival mechanism — it has proven itself as exactly that. But because opposition does not explain existence. It only defends it. And defence, however necessary and however real, is not the same as justification.

It is possible to remain alive through unresolved accountability, through refusal to concede, through the stubborn determination not to hand one's enemies a cheap victory — and still not have answered the question underneath. These reasons are not false. They are not meaningless. They have held, in the specific ways and in the specific moments where nothing else did. But they are not complete. They hold a person in place. They do not fully tell them why that place should be held.

And at some point — not theoretically, but practically, in the specific experience of a person who has been carrying this question long enough — that distinction begins to matter. Because what the investigation has been looking for since Chapter 9's anchor redefinition is something that holds even when there is nothing left to push against. Something that does not depend on the continued presence of an enemy, a fear, a barrier, or a refusal. Something that remains when opposition has exhausted itself.

Defiance brought the investigation here. It is not what the investigation has been looking for. But it was real enough, and honest enough, and stubborn enough to keep the search alive long enough to continue.

That is not nothing. That is, in its own unglamorous way, everything.

CHAPTER 16 — *When Something Begins to Hold*

Jonas had not been looking for it. That was the detail he kept returning to afterwards, because it seemed to matter in a way he could not fully account for.

He was a structural engineer. His professional formation had given him a specific relationship with evidence: things held, or they did not, and the question of whether they held was answered by calculation, by testing, by the accumulated record of what materials did under load. He had no particular hostility to religious belief — he had no use for it. It occupied a category in his thinking that he associated with comfort rather than truth, with the management of uncertainty rather than its honest acknowledgement.

He was forty-nine when the period of sustained difficulty began. He would not have called it a crisis in any dramatic sense. It was quieter than that — a gradual erosion of the things that had previously carried enough weight to keep the question at a manageable distance. The work was still there. The relationships were still there. The frameworks he had built for understanding his life were still, technically, intact. But they had stopped functioning in the way they previously had. The weight they were being asked to carry exceeded what they could hold.

He was not, at this point, seeking anything. He was managing. Doing what had always worked, with diminishing returns, and not yet ready to name what that meant.

What happened next, he has described in different ways at different times, and the descriptions have never quite satisfied him. Not because he is uncertain about what happened. Because language consistently falls short of it. Something arrived that was not a thought. It did not behave like information. It did not remain external. It engaged — not only with his mind but with something underneath his mind, at the level where the weight actually lived. And it did not, when he subsequently subjected it to the analytical habits of thirty years of professional training, dissolve.

He did not know what to call it. He was not sure the available vocabulary was adequate. But he was, after it, a person who was holding something he had not been holding before. And what he was holding had not come from inside him.

By this point in the search, something has already been established — not as a conclusion but as a boundary. Some things help a person continue. And there are things that answer why they should. The two are not the same. Everything examined so far has belonged, in one way or another, to the first category. Some have been strong. Some necessary. Some, at times, are indispensable. None has fully met the second.

Which means that if anything is to be called an anchor in the sense the investigation has required since Chapter 9 — something that holds not by managing the weight of life but by giving a reason to carry it — it must be something different. Not another variation of what has already been tested, but something that appears where those things do not hold.

It is at this point that a pattern begins to come into view. Not constructed. Observed. Across different lives, different contexts, different starting points. And what is consistent in the pattern is not its uniformity — the language used to describe it varies considerably — but its structure. Something is encountered. Not reasoned into existence. Not constructed from available materials. Encountered. And what is encountered does something that the previously examined anchors did not: it does not depend on improved circumstances, emotional stability, or intellectual clarity to remain present.

The investigation examines three accounts — chosen not because they are the only available ones, but because each comes from a person with every intellectual and temperamental credential to dismiss what they encountered, and who subsequently found they could not.

Blaise Pascal was among the most rigorous analytical minds of the seventeenth century — a mathematician, physicist, inventor, and a person for whom the quality of evidence was not an abstract concern but a professional commitment. On the night of 23 November 1654, he experienced something he documented in a fragment now known as the *Memorial*. It begins with a single word written in capitals: *FIRE*. It continues not as a theological argument but as a record — urgent, personal, resistant to paraphrase. He did not publish it. He did not perform it. He sewed it into the lining of his coat and wore it against his body until his death eight years later, transferring it to each new coat as the previous one wore out. [1] That is not the behaviour of a man who adopted a comforting idea. That is the behaviour of a man who encountered something he considered too important to lose and too private to display. The analytical mind that had built the foundations of probability theory found, in this encounter, something that did not behave like a probability. It behaved like a presence.

C.S. Lewis arrived at belief by a route he described, with characteristic precision, as reluctant. He was not a person inclined toward religious sentiment. He was a literary scholar and philosopher who had spent his adult life without faith and without a particular desire for it. What changed was not a decision. It was, in his own account, an encounter with something that had been pursuing him — the image he used, in *Surprised by Joy*, was of a person who had been running from something until the running became no longer possible. [2] What is analytically significant is not the theological content of his account but its structural character: he did not describe adopting an idea. He described being confronted by something he could no longer dismiss. The distinction is the same one that the investigation has been drawing throughout this chapter.

Francis Collins directed the Human Genome Project — the scientific undertaking that mapped the complete sequence of human DNA — and served as Director of the National Institutes of Health. He documented his conversion from committed atheism in *The Language of God* (2006), describing a specific moment during a hike in the Cascade Mountains — not a church, not a theological argument, not a community — in which something arrived that his scientific formation gave him no framework to accommodate and his analytical habits gave him no mechanism to dismiss subsequently. [3] Collins is a contemporary witness to the same structural pattern: encounter rather than construction, arrival rather than adoption, persistence under examination rather than dissolution on contact with scrutiny.

The investigation must be precise here because it would be easy, at this point, to move too quickly — to name what is being observed before it has been fully examined, to assign it meaning before the examination is complete.

What the investigation can say at this stage, from the evidence of the pattern, is this: something is being encountered in these accounts that does not behave like the other anchors examined. It does not depend on the continued presence of favourable conditions. It does not require the maintenance of a particular intellectual framework. It does not dissolve when scrutinised by the same minds that constructed rigorous analytical frameworks in other domains.

Whether this is a psychological adaptation, a form of meaning-making under existential pressure, or something that exceeds those categories, the investigation has not yet answered. Research into religious and existential conversion has noted that under conditions of crisis, individuals can undergo shifts not easily explained by incremental reasoning alone, consistently describing the experience in terms of encounter rather than conclusion. [4] That finding does not settle the question. It confirms that the question is real, that the pattern is documented, and that what is being observed is not an anomaly but a recurrence — across cultures, centuries, and intellectual starting points — that deserves to be taken seriously on its own terms.

What the investigation can also say, from the standard established in Chapter 9, is that what is being observed in these accounts appears to meet conditions that nothing else examined has met. It does not remove difficulty. It prevents collapse. It does not answer every question. It changes their weight. It does not eliminate uncertainty. It does not depend on certainty to remain either.

Jonas, the structural engineer, returned to his work. The professional formation was still there. The analytical habits were still there. What had changed was not his capacity to examine evidence — it was, if anything, sharpened by what had happened — but his relationship to the weight he had been carrying. The weight had not gone. But something was holding that had not been holding before. And that something had not come from inside him. He knew the difference, as a structural engineer, between a load-bearing element and a non-load-bearing one. What had arrived was bearing weight he had not been able to bear himself.

He still did not have adequate language for it. He suspected he never would. But inadequate language for something real is not the same as evidence that the thing is not there.

The investigation has not concluded. Recognition is not a conclusion. To say *this appears to hold* is not the same as saying *this is the answer.* The distinction matters — and the investigation will hold it.

But the question is no longer being asked in the same way it has been asked since Chapter 1. It has narrowed. It has sharpened. It is no longer asking whether anything exists that meets the anchor standard. It is asking what exactly it is that, in these accounts and in the biographical material this investigation has been carrying throughout, appears to meet it.

That question has a name. The investigation has been approached across sixteen chapters. The next chapter will not avoid it any longer.

CHAPTER 17 — *When the Anchor Is No Longer Avoided*

Ama had not arrived at this point by choice. That was what she kept returning to when she tried to account for it afterwards — not that she had decided, or concluded, or been persuaded, but that she had run out of other places to stand.

The process had taken years. Not a dramatic arc but an accumulating one — the quiet exhaustion of each available framework, one after another, in the specific order that her life had presented them. She had tried, in good faith, the things that the people around her recommended. The therapy had been useful until it reached the border of its operational range. The philosophical frameworks she had built had held until they encountered the weight that they were not designed to carry. The relationships were real and remained, but they could not cross the distance between what she was experiencing internally and what any external presence could reach.

She was not, when the shift occurred, in a condition of openness. She was in a condition of depletion. Every resource she had trusted had been found, through sustained testing rather than casual assessment, to fall short at the same point. She had not been looking for what arrived. She would not have known how to look for it. What she knew was that she had run out of alternatives — and that running out of alternatives is a different state from being ready to receive something.

What arrived did not behave like a thought. It did not behave like a conclusion. It behaved, and she used this word reluctantly because she knew how it sounded, like a person meeting her where she actually was — not where she presented herself to be, not where the frameworks assumed she was, but where she actually was, at the level where the weight lived.

She did not immediately know what to call it. She was not sure the available vocabulary was adequate. But she knew, with the certainty of a person who had spent years testing what held and what did not, that what had arrived was bearing weight she had not been able to bear herself. And that it had not come from inside her.

By this point in the investigation, the search is no longer open-ended. It is constrained — not by preference, but by the accumulated record of what has been examined and where each thing has failed.

The summary is precise:

Pleasure helps, but resets under pressure. Achievement structures but requires continuous maintenance. Relationships sustain, but remain contingent on conditions outside one's control. Control stabilises, but fluctuates with the internal state it is designed to regulate. Meaning frameworks interpret, but depend on the cognitive clarity to sustain them. Clinical intervention restores function, but it was never designed to answer why function should be restored. The defiance of remaining — real, documented, personally operative — holds without answering. Identity and ideology organise, but depend on the continuity of recognition and framework integrity.

Each has contributed. None has qualified. And the standard against which they have been measured — established in Chapter 9 and held without revision since — remains unchanged: something that holds not by managing the weight of life but by giving a reason to carry it. Something that does not depend on improved circumstances, emotional stability, or the individual's capacity to sustain it. Something that remains when nothing else does.

Under that standard, something has already appeared, not as a conclusion — the investigation makes no conclusions — but as a pattern, observed across multiple accounts in the preceding chapter. Individuals under conditions of collapse, with every intellectual credential to dismiss what they encountered, described something that arrived rather than being constructed, that persisted rather than dissolving under scrutiny, that did not behave like the other anchors because it did not depend on the individual sustaining it.

The pattern has a feature that everything previously examined lacks. It is described, consistently and across different cultural and historical contexts, as personal. Not a system. Not a framework. Not a presence-in-general. But something encountered as a person encounters another person — specifically, responsively, in a way that is not reducible to internal psychological process.

This is the point at which the investigation can no longer remain general. It must become specific. Because what the investigation is approaching has a name, and the investigation has been approaching it across seventeen chapters precisely by not naming it prematurely.

Before the name is given, the biographical record of this investigation must be laid out in full because the investigation has not been conducted from a position of detachment. It has been conducted from inside the question, by a specific person, with a specific history, who has been carrying this question for longer than any of the clinical or philosophical frameworks encountered along the way.

I was a young telecoms engineer in Port Harcourt, in my bachelorhood years, more than seventeen years before any clinical diagnosis would arrive. I remember the feeling with a vividness that time has not reduced. Not thoughts. Not plans. A recurring wish that the earth were flat, so I could keep walking until I dropped off the edge. No violence in the image. No destination. Only the wish for a continuation that eventually ran out — a walking that went on long enough to be relieved of the burden of my turning back. I had no language for it then. The question was present before I had any of the frameworks this book has examined. It preceded the diagnosis. It preceded the clinical history. It preceded everything.

Years later, in London, I found myself reading consent forms for First-in-Human clinical trials — studies that introduce untested compounds into a healthy body to establish toxicity thresholds. The consent forms itemised the risks with clinical precision. I read them... The official language calls it volunteering. I called it survival — survival for others, specifically. The money would support my family. And within that calculus, the risk to myself was not the troubling part. It was, in a way I could only name later through Joiner's framework, the point. My existence as a currency. My body is a contribution more useful than my continuation of living.

I said, at the point where that anecdote first entered this investigation, that things changed — not because circumstances improved, but because something else reached the question first.

This is the chapter where that can be named.

What has actually held across Port Harcourt, across London, across the decades in between, across the full span of conditions this investigation has examined, is not any of the anchors the preceding chapters found insufficient. It has not been primarily pleasure, achievement, career, relationship, identity, control, culture, escape, meaning, or clinical stabilisation. These have all contributed, in their specific ways, to the survivability of my search. None of them is what has held at the point where holding was most required.

What has held is more accurately described in the terms I have been circling since the Author's Note, and which must now be stated directly.

I have been a Christian for longer than the struggle has lasted. That is not a comfortable thing to write in this context, because the faith tradition I was formed in tends toward explanation. Suffering is attributed. Causes are named. The appropriate response is spiritual warfare, deliverance, and the casting out of what has been identified as the source. I understand that framework. I'm shaped by it. And I have come to believe, through the specific suffering this book is about, that it does not always reach what it claims to address. Not because the faith is wrong. Because the explanation is insufficient, there is a difference — a categorical one — between a faith that explains suffering and a faith that sustains within suffering. The first offers a reason for the weight. The second offers a presence within it. I did not find, in the explanations, what the question required. The second is what I mean when I speak of what has held.

Martin Luther King Jr. knew this distinction from the inside. In January 1956 — at the height of the Montgomery Bus Boycott, after a death threat had arrived by phone in the small hours — he sat alone at his kitchen table on the verge of abandoning everything. By his own account, documented in *Stride Toward Freedom,* he prayed — not as a performed religious act but as the last available action of a man who had exhausted every other resource. What he described as arriving in that moment was not a theological argument. Not a reframing of his circumstances. Not a recovered sense of purpose. A presence — specific, felt, personal — that gave him what he later said was the courage to continue. He did not overcome his depression that night. He did not resolve the threat. What changed was that something was holding that had not been holding before. He was not alone in the kitchen in the way he had been alone when he sat down. [1]

That is not proof. It is a witness. A man who had known the question since childhood — who had carried depression across decades of public life, who had refused clinical intervention, whose ideological anchor was visibly strained under the weight of a movement in crisis — found, at the point of genuine exhaustion of every personal resource, something that held. Not an idea. A person meeting him where he actually was.

The faith tradition this investigation has arrived at does not spiritualise what has not been resolved. It does not resolve the weight to a demonic cause and offers deliverance as the lone remedy. What it offers is something the ancient text names with a precision that no contemporary framework has matched.

The prophet Habakkuk wrote from within conditions of sustained difficulty and the complete absence of visible reason for hope. The passage that has been the background note of this investigation since the memoir was first written closes with words that are not triumphant — they are defiant in the specific way that Chapter 15 identified as the most honest available posture under sustained pressure:

"Yet I will rejoice in the Lord, I will joy in the God of my salvation." [2]

The operative word is *yet*. Not *because*. Not *therefore*. Not *now that*. Yet. The fig tree has not budded. The flocks are not in the fields. Nothing has been resolved. And yet — not despite the absence of resolution, but within it, from inside it, without waiting for it — the posture holds. This is not the language of a person who has found an answer. It is the language of a person who has found something that holds in the absence of an answer. The distinction is the anchor.

The investigation must now name what it has found — not as a conclusion, not as a proof, but as the honest account of what the search has arrived at.

In the Gospel of John, Jesus makes a claim that the investigation has been approaching for seventeen chapters. It is not a claim about a system, a framework, or an accumulated body of wisdom. It is a claim of personal identity:

"I am the way, the truth, and the life." [3]

The grammar is not incidental. Not *I show the way*. I do not *explain the truth*. Not *I give life*. The claim is first-person and present-tense and unmediated. It is the claim of a person — not a method, not an idea, not a framework — identifying themselves as what the search has been looking for.

A second statement in the same account reframes what the search itself has been doing:

"Ye will not come to me, that ye might have life." [4]

This is a structural observation. Not: *life is not available*. But: *life is being sought in what testifies about me rather than in me directly*. The Scriptures, the frameworks, the accumulated wisdom — these are documents pointing toward a person. The investigation has been examining the documents. What this statement claims is that the person is not the document.

The claim must be tested against the established standard. Has what has been encountered — across Port Harcourt, across London, across the kitchen table in Montgomery, across the accounts of Pascal and

Lewis and Collins and the long record of individuals who encountered rather than constructed — meet the criteria?

Is it encountered rather than constructed? The biographical record and the pattern of accounts say: yes. Is it independent of circumstance? The record of what has held when circumstances did not improve says: yes. Is it not dependent on the individual's internal state? The specific experience of emotional encasement — a pressure that does not respond to reasoning — having been met by something that does not require clarity to arrive says: yes. Does it remain under pressure? Seventeen chapters of honest examination, across decades of a specific person's specific struggle, say: yes.

This does not constitute proof. No honest investigation claims proof for what cannot be empirically verified. What it constitutes is the finding of a search conducted without a predetermined destination, across the full range of available alternatives, arriving at the only remaining option that has not been found insufficient.

The search has not found an idea. It has found someone—a person.

I said in Chapter 15 that what has held, on certain days, is defiance — the refusal to hand my enemies (howsoever defined) a cheap victory. Also, I said that the theological barrier — the anxiety to optimally please the God (יהוה) I am entirely convinced exists — has functioned, in the darkest moments, as a fence. These things are true, and I do not retract them. They have held in the ways they have held. But they are not the anchor. They are, on reflection, the traces of a relationship whose full character I have not always been able to access — a relationship with the God (יהוה) who is real enough to be feared, who means well enough to be present, who is well able enough to meet what nothing else has reached.

The cowardice, on examination, was not primarily fear of judgment. It was the trace of a conviction about God's reality that was operating even when the conscious relationship to that reality was at its most strained periods. And the defiance — *live against if you cannot live for* — was, on reflection, the most honest expression available to a person who had not yet fully articulated what they were refusing to surrender to. The enemy logic contained, underneath itself, a prior logic: that there was something worth protecting. That continuation mattered to something beyond the self.

I am not writing from the other side of this. The Author's Note was true and remains true. The weight has not fully lifted. The question has not been finally resolved. Habakkuk's *yet* is the honest position — not arrival, not rescue, but defiant continuation within the ongoing conditions, held by something that does not depend on the conditions improving.

That is not a triumph. It is, in the most honest terms available, what the search has found.

CHAPTER 18 — *Testing the Person Directly*

Reuben had spent his professional life in evidence, not as an abstraction — as a daily discipline. He was a research scientist, and the question of what constituted sufficient grounds for a conclusion was not philosophical for him. It was procedural. You did not accept what you could not test. You did not conclude what the data did not support. You did not, under any circumstances, mistake the plausibility of an idea for confirmation of its truth.

He had applied this discipline to every framework the preceding years had brought him into contact with. He had found, through sustained application rather than casual assessment, that each one reached a border it could not cross. The frameworks were real. The border was real. The gap between what they provided and what the question required was real. He had not dismissed any of them cheaply. He had found, honestly, that none of them was sufficient.

What he had not done — what his formation had made structurally difficult — was to apply the same discipline to the possibility that the investigation had now arrived at. Not because he considered it beneath examination. But because the nature of the test was different, and different tests made him uncomfortable. He was good at external verification. He was less certain about what it meant to test something that, by its own account, required encounter to evaluate.

He sat with that discomfort for a long time before he recognised it as the last honest move available. Not faith. Not conversion. The recognition that a person cannot be evaluated from a distance — and that remaining at a distance, in the name of rigour, was itself a choice with consequences.

He had been rigorous about everything else. He would be rigorous about this, too.

The investigation is not finished. It has identified what the search has been looking for — not a framework or a system or an accumulated body of wisdom, but a person making a specific and total claim about what life is and where it is found. Identification is not validation. Nothing in this investigation has been accepted because it appeared meaningful. Everything has been tested. Whatever now stands must be tested in the same way.

The nature of the test, however, must change. And understanding why it must change is itself the chapter's first analytical task.

A framework can be examined from the outside itself. A method can be applied and the results observed. A system can be stress-tested by probing its internal consistency against cases it was not designed to handle. All of the anchors examined in this investigation have been tested in these ways — externally, analytically, against the specific standard established in Chapter 9.

But a person — and the investigation has already named Him: Jesus Christ —cannot be tested in the same way. Not because they are beyond scrutiny — the claim being examined is radical enough that scrutiny is exactly what it requires. But because the question changes. The test of a framework is: *does this work when applied?* The test of a person is: *does this remain when encountered?* And those are different questions requiring different forms of investigation. One can be conducted from a distance. The other cannot.

This does not reduce the rigour. It relocates it. What follows is the most rigorous examination this investigation has conducted — precisely because the claim being examined is the most absolute it has encountered.

The historical question. The claim under examination is not presented as abstract philosophy. It is embedded in first-century historical narrative — accounts that name specific people, specific places, specific dates, and that were written within the living memory of the events they describe. Richard Bauckham's detailed examination of the Gospel accounts argues that they reflect eyewitness testimony rather than legendary development — that the specificity of named individuals, the counterintuitive details, and the pattern of what is included and omitted is consistent with the behaviour of eyewitness memory rather than mythological construction. [1]

This does not prove the claims. But it establishes something the investigation requires: that the subject of the claim is not, in the simple sense, fictional. Which means the question cannot be dismissed at the level of myth. The historical question pushes the examination to a harder level: not only *did this person exist,* but *do the claims made about and by this person correspond to reality?* That is the question the remaining tests are designed to address.

The psychological question. This is the most serious intellectual challenge to the investigation's finding, and it deserves the most honest treatment. The objection is coherent: under conditions of collapse, the human mind generates meaning to preserve itself. What is described as *an encounter may be emotional compensation, cognitive restructuring, or neurological relief* — *an internal process experienced as an* external presence. If that is what is being observed, then it belongs in the same category as the previously examined anchors: genuinely helpful, genuinely insufficient.

The investigation takes this objection seriously. It cannot be dismissed. What it can do is note what the most qualified witnesses have observed about the distinction. Pascal — whose professional formation was built on the exact question of what constitutes sufficient grounds for a conclusion — subjected what happened on the night of 23 November 1654 to exactly this scrutiny. He did not immediately publish it, perform it, or build a public identity around it. He sewed it into his coat and wore it against his skin. The behaviour of a man managing an internal process is a public declaration. The behaviour of a man carrying something he considers too important to display is private custody. Collins — whose scientific standing rests on the quality of his relationship to evidence — applied his analytical habits to what he encountered in the Cascade Mountains and found, to his own documented surprise, that it did not dissolve under examination. King, alone at a kitchen table in January 1956, described what arrived as having the specific quality of not being his own — of coming from outside the system that was failing. [2]

Research into religious and experiential encounters has noted that what distinguishes these accounts from purely internal construction is precisely their sense of *otherness* — the consistent description of something arriving that the person did not generate and could not fully account for within their existing cognitive framework. [3] This does not settle the matter. It prevents premature dismissal. And it places the burden of proof on both sides: the objection must account for why the most analytically rigorous witnesses consistently describe something that does not behave like an internal process.

In my own experience — the encasement that does not respond to reasoning, that is not generated by cognition and therefore not reached by cognitive intervention — what has arrived at the point of most sustained pressure has had exactly this quality of otherness. It has not felt like my own resources reassembling. It has felt like something meeting me at the level where the weight actually lives, from outside the system that was failing. I cannot prove that distinction. But I know the difference between the two — and the difference is the investigation's most important biographical data point.

The durability question. The central test. Not whether these comforts — comfort is available from multiple sources and has been found insufficient. Instead, whether it remains when circumstances do not improve. Whether the pressure continues and the anchor holds, regardless.

The biographical record of this investigation covers more than three decades — from Port Harcourt to London to the present — during which the conditions generating the question have not consistently improved. The clinical history has been what it has been. The struggle has been sustained rather than episodic. The weight has not been lifted in any final sense.

What has remained, across that span, is not any of the frameworks the preceding chapters examined. It is the thing Chapter 17 named — a presence that does not depend on the conditions improving to remain present. The Habakkuk position: *yet*, not because the fig tree has budded, but in its continued absence. That *has yet to be* operative across thirty-plus years of a specific person's specific struggles. It is the investigation's most direct available evidence of durability under the exact conditions the test requires. [4]

The dependence question. Every previous anchor required the individual to sustain it. The Stoic framework required cognitive clarity. The identity anchor required continuity of recognition. The meaning framework required the will to maintain the construction. Clinical stabilisation required compliance and access. Even defiance required something to push against.

The claim being tested is structurally different. It does not claim that the individual sustains the relationship. It claims Jesus Christ remains regardless, independently of whether the individual is capable of sustaining anything. That distinction shifts the burden of stability from the person carrying the weight to the person claimed to be holding them. If the claim is true, the anchor does not fluctuate with the individual's internal state. It holds when the internal state is at its most depleted — which is precisely when the question the book has been pursuing presses hardest.

The test for this claim cannot be conducted analytically. It requires exactly what Reuben eventually recognised: that remaining at a distance, in the name of rigour, is itself a choice. A person cannot be tested except by encounter. And encounter requires a movement that analysis alone cannot make.

The limits question. Every anchor examined in this investigation has limits. The honest test of the final anchor is not whether it has none, but whether it collapses under its genuine challenges.

The challenges are real. Why does suffering remain if the anchor holds? Why is clarity not constant? Why is the encounter not universally uniform? Why do some people, in apparently similar conditions, not describe what others describe? These are not peripheral questions. They are central. And the investigation will not answer them by deflection.

What can be said honestly is this: the claim under examination does not promise the removal of suffering. The 2 Corinthians passage examined in Chapter 14 — *pressed but not crushed, perplexed but not driven to despair* — is not a description of suffering's removal. It is a description of something holding within it. Habakkuk *yet* is not a resolution. It is a posture maintained in unresolved conditions. The claim is not that the anchor eliminates the weight. The claim is that it prevents the weight from having the final word.

Whether that is sufficient depends on what the question has actually been asking. If the question is *why suffering exists,* the anchor does not answer it. If the question is *why continue when suffering does not resolve*, the anchor addresses exactly that. The investigation has been asking the second question since Chapter 1. And the honest finding is that, against the second question, what has been found does not collapse under examination.

It holds. Not by eliminating what presses. By outlasting it.

At this point, the investigation reaches its limit — not of honesty, but of method. Every other anchor has been testable from the outside. This one is not fully testable from the outside. Not because it is beyond scrutiny — the preceding tests have applied scrutiny without exception — but because what is being tested is a person. A person's reliability cannot be finally verified without relational engagement. Analysis can bring the reader to the threshold. It cannot cross it on their behalf.

This introduces what is, at the close of eighteen chapters, the only question the investigation cannot answer for the reader.

Will I come close enough to find out — close enough to the person the investigation has named, Jesus Christ, to test what cannot be tested from a distance?

Not: *is this true in the abstract?* Not: *does the evidence suggest a valid conclusion?* But: *will I take the step that cannot be taken analytically — the step toward engagement with the person rather than assessment of a claim?*

That question cannot be answered in abstraction. The investigation has done what investigations can do: it has followed the question honestly, tested every available alternative against the established standard, and arrived at the only remaining option that has not been found insufficient. It has laid the biographical record open — including the parts that are not flattering, not resolved, not complete. It has not concluded. It has reported what the search has actually found.

What happens next is not for the investigation to determine. It is for the readers to ascertain.

Reuben, the research scientist, eventually made the move he had been resisting. Not because the analytical questions had been fully resolved — they had not. But because he recognised that remaining at a distance indefinitely, on the grounds that the test required proximity he had not yet established, was not rigorous. It was avoidance wearing rigour's clothing. He had spent three years finding that everything else failed at the same point. The one remaining honest move was to test what he had not yet tested — not from a distance, but at the range the test required.

He did not find what he expected. He is not sure, even now, that he has adequate language for what he found. But he knows the difference — as a scientist, professionally — between a load-bearing element and a non-load-bearing one. What he encountered was bearing weight that nothing in his own system had been able to bear. And it had not come from inside his system.

That is not proof. It is testimony. And testimony, in the specific conditions this investigation has been examining, is sometimes the most precise form of evidence available.

CHAPTER 19 — *The Anchor That Holds*

Amara had not arrived anywhere; she would call resolved.

That was the first thing she said when asked, sometime after the period the previous chapter described, what had changed. Not: *I found the answer.* Not: *the weight lifted.* What she said was more specific and, in its specificity, more honest than either of those.

Something is holding that was not holding before. I cannot fully account for it. But I know the difference between being held and not being held. And the difference is real.

The search had not ended. But something had changed in how it was being conducted. She was no longer searching from a position of complete depletion — the position from which the search had, for a long time, been conducted. She was searching from a position of being accompanied. Not by an idea. Not by a framework. By something she had no fully adequate language for and had largely stopped trying to force into the categories that did not quite fit.

The weight was still present. The questions were still open. The conditions had not dramatically improved. But she was, in a way she could not have predicted from inside the depletion, still here. And the difference between still being here and not being here was not, she had come to understand, nothing.

It was everything that made continuing possible.

This is the last entry in the investigation. Not because every question has been answered — several have not, and the chapter will not pretend otherwise. But because everything that can be examined from within the search has been examined. The investigation has followed the question as far as the investigation can follow it. What remains cannot be completed in writing. It must be faced individually, by each person who has arrived here, in whatever condition they have arrived.

Before turning to the reader, the investigation owes one final honest account of its own position.

I began the journey of this book as a young telecoms engineer in Port Harcourt, in my bachelorhood years, more than seventeen years before any clinical language would arrive to name what was already present. I remember wishing the earth were flat — not as a thought I could argue with, but as a feeling that recurred, specific and persistent: if the earth were flat, I could keep walking until I dropped off the edge. Not violent. Not planned. Only the wish for a continuation that eventually ran out. I had no language for it then. I had no framework. I had, in fact, none of the anchors this investigation has spent eighteen chapters examining. The question was present before all of them.

It has been present since.

I am writing this not from the other side of the question — the Author's Note said as much, and it remains true. I am writing it from inside the question, at a point further along the road than Port Harcourt, than London, than the clinical diagnosis of a decade ago, even earlier than when I had hoped that risking my body for First-In-Human studies might be worth more than my continuation of living. I am writing from a position in which something has been found that holds — not by resolving the conditions that generated the question, but by remaining present within them. The Habakkuk position: *yet*. Not because the fig tree has budded. In its continued absence. A defiant, unglamorous, sustained *yet* that is not triumph and is not rescue but is, in the most honest terms available, the finding of this investigation.

What has been found is not a method, not a framework, not a system to maintain. It is a person encountered rather than constructed, present when the capacity to sustain anything else has been depleted, bearing weight that nothing in my own system has been able to bear. I cannot prove this. The investigation has acknowledged that from the beginning. What I can report is that the thirty-year longitudinal account of a specific person's specific struggle — from Port Harcourt through London through the present — has found, at the point where every other available thing has reached its border, one thing that has not reached that border. And that finding is what this book has been built to report.

I am not resolved. I am accompanied. And in the specific conditions this investigation has examined, those are different words for something real.

The investigation has now traced a full arc. What follows is the summary — not as a list, but as the honest account of what the search found at each point.

Pleasure was examined and found real but impermanent — it resets under pressure and cannot bear the weight it was never designed to carry. Achievement was examined and found real but contingent — it requires continuous maintenance and collapses when the maintenance is no longer possible. Relationships were examined and found real but finite — they sustain under conditions that cannot be guaranteed and can, under sustained distress, invert their own function. Identity and ideology were examined and found real but dependent on continuity of recognition and framework integrity that crisis disrupts. Control and regulation were examined and found real but insufficient — they stabilise the surface without reaching the question underneath. Escape and numbing were examined and found real but structurally opposed to what an anchor must do — creating distance rather than presence. Meaning frameworks were examined and found real but cognitively bounded — they cannot operate below the level of thought they require to sustain them. Clinical stabilisation was examined and found real and necessary, and insufficient — it creates conditions under which the search can continue, but was never designed to answer what the search is looking for. The defiance of remaining — the *live against* when the *live for* has failed — was examined and found real and operative and incomplete: it holds without explaining, resists without grounding, and depends on the continued presence of something to push against.

None of these failed. None answered the question completely. Each belongs in a life — contributes to survivability, to function, to the maintenance of the search. None is the anchor in the sense required by the investigation.

What the investigation found, at the end of this sequence, was a pattern across multiple accounts — historical, biographical, contemporary — of something encountered rather than constructed, personal rather than conceptual, present rather than dependent on the individual's capacity to maintain it. The pattern was tested against the established standard. Its claims were examined. Its limits were acknowledged honestly. Its objections were taken seriously rather than deflected. The result was not an absolute resolution — the investigation has claimed no such thing. The result was that, against the standard applied consistently across nineteen chapters, this was the only thing examined that did not fail at the same point at which everything else failed.

That is what has been found. Not proven in the abstract. Observed, tested, and left standing.

And this is where the investigation must address the reader directly — because you have been the investigation's companion since the first chapter, and you are owed an honest accounting of where the search has arrived for each person who reads these words.

If you have reached this point and found nothing that holds — if the investigation's finding has not corresponded to anything in your own experience, and the search remains unresolved — the question remains open. It has not been closed by this investigation. The investigation cannot close it for you. What it can say is that an open question is not an answered one, and the search is worth continuing. The fact that you followed it this far is itself evidence that you are still looking. Looking is not nothing.

If you have recognised something in the investigation's finding that corresponds to something in your own experience — something that has held in conditions where other things did not, something that arrived rather than being constructed, something that you have perhaps not yet allowed yourself to name — the question becomes whether you will move toward it. Not in a leap. Not in the abandonment of everything the investigation has established about honest examination.

But in the recognition that a person or *'presence'* cannot be evaluated from a distance indefinitely. At some point, the honest move is the one that requires proximity.

If you are uncertain — if the investigation has brought you to a threshold without bringing you across it, if you can see what might be there without yet being able to say it is — that uncertainty is not a failure. It is the most honest position available to a person who has followed the question with integrity. The investigation began in uncertainty. It has not ended in certainty. What it has found is something worth the continued examination. Uncertainty, in the presence of something worth examining, is not the end of the search. It is the search continuing in its most honest form.

The investigation closes with what it has always tried to be: an honest account of a search that is still underway, conducted by a specific person who has not arrived anywhere he would call finished, who has found someone he would call real, and who cannot complete the search on anyone else's behalf.

The young telecoms engineer in Port Harcourt, who wished the earth were flat so he could walk until he dropped off the edge, is still walking. The Earth is not flat. The edge has not arrived. Someone has been accompanying the walk that was not there at the beginning, or was there, and could not yet be named. He has been named now. His name is Jesus Christ.

The question that began this investigation — *Why stay alive?* — has not been answered in the form it was first asked. What has been found instead is something more demanding and more honest than an answer: a presence within the question that makes continuing possible without requiring the question to first resolve.

That is the anchor.

It holds.

Not by removing the weight.

By being stronger than whatever weight.

The search belongs to you now.

A note from the author: If anything in this book has brought you to a point of acute distress rather than reflection, please do not remain there alone. The crisis resources listed on the copyright page are available. Professional care — therapy, clinical support, honest conversation with a doctor — is not a retreat from the search. It is, as this investigation has said from the beginning, often what makes the search survivable. The investigation is not a substitute for that care. It is a companion to it.

EPILOGUE — *His Name Is Jesus*

The investigation is complete. But before this book closes, something must be said that the preceding chapters approached and did not say clearly enough.

The anchor has a name.

Across nineteen chapters, the search examined everything that human beings reach for when life implodes — pleasure, achievement, relationship, identity, control, escape, meaning, clinical stabilisation, defiance, the accumulated wisdom of centuries — and found each of them, in the specific conditions the book has been examining, insufficient. Not worthless. Insufficient. Real contributions to survivability. Not one of them is strong enough to hold at the point where holding is most required.

And then something was found that held.

Something encountered rather than constructed.

Something personal rather than conceptual.

Something that remained when nothing else did.

That something is someone. And that someone is Jesus Christ.

The investigation has been honest enough to name everything else it found. It owes the reader the same honesty at the end. If the anchor had been a product, a protocol, or a philosophy, it would have been named without hesitation. The anchor is a person. His name is Jesus Christ. And He has already spoken, in the most precise available language, to the exact condition this book has been describing.

"Come unto me, all ye that labour and are heavy laden, and I will give you rest."
— Matthew 11:28

That is not a doctrinal statement. That is a direct address. To the person who has been carrying a weight that nothing else has been able to carry. To the person who has exhausted what the preceding chapters examined — and perhaps more besides. To the person who has arrived at this page still inside the question, still under the weight, still uncertain whether anything holds.

Come. Not: agree to a theological position. Not: join an institution. Not: resolve every question first. Not: arrive in better condition. Come. As you are. Where you are. With the weight you are carrying. The invitation does not require the weight to be gone before it is accepted.

It requires only the step.

The step is not complicated. It is simply this: tell Him where you are. Not in the language of formal prayer, if that language is not available to you. In whatever language is honest. The person who sat alone at a kitchen table in Montgomery in 1956 and said what was true — that he was afraid, that he was depleted, that he could not continue alone — found that something arrived in response that he could not account for except as presence. Not a feeling he generated. A presence that met him. That is still available. It has not been withdrawn.

You do not need to have everything resolved before you take the step. You do not need to feel ready. You do not need to be certain. What the investigation has established is that certainty is not the condition for encounter. Proximity is. And proximity begins with the smallest honest movement toward the person who has already said, "come."

If you are in a place where continuing feels impossible — where the weight is at its most acute — please also use the crisis resources on the copyright page. The step toward Jesus Christ and the step toward clinical support are not in competition with one another. This investigation has maintained that from the Author's Note. Both are available. Both matter. Neither cancels the other.

But this Epilogue exists to say, without qualification, what the investigation found:

The anchor is real. The anchor holds. The anchor's name is Jesus Christ. And He is not waiting for you to be better before He receives you. He is waiting for you to come.

"Come unto me."

That is the invitation. It has been standing for two thousand years. It is standing now.

What you do with it is, as this investigation has always maintained, down to you.

Acknowledgements

This book was written alone and through loneliness, which is an accurate description of both the writing and the question it investigates.

The people who could be named here know who they are, even where the complexity of what has been shared between us resists the conventions of acknowledgement.

The anchor named in these pages has been present throughout. That requires no elaboration here.

Discussion Guide

This guide is designed for individuals reading alone, in small groups, in book clubs, in university seminars, in pastoral study groups, and in mental health peer support communities. It does not assume a particular conclusion has been reached. It assumes only that the reader has followed the investigation honestly and is willing to continue doing so in conversation.

The guide is organised around the book's five natural movements rather than its nineteen chapters. Each movement contains six to eight questions and a brief note indicating what the question is designed to surface. The questions move from observation to reflection to personal application — following the same progression the investigation itself followed.

A note on safety: some of the questions in this guide engage directly with experiences of despair, suicidal feelings, and the limits of conventional support. If you are using this guide in a group setting, it is recommended that a facilitator establish at the outset that no one is required to disclose more than they choose to, that professional support resources are available (see the copyright page of the book), and that the conversation is held with the same honesty and without the same pressure to resolve that the book itself maintained.

The guide does not close the search. Neither did the book. What follows is a structure for continuing it — together, or alone, or both.

How to Use This Guide

Each movement can be used as a standalone session or as part of a five-session series. A single session works well at ninety minutes to two hours, allowing approximately fifteen to twenty minutes per question at a relaxed pace. For groups who wish to go deeper, each movement contains enough material for a full two-hour session with selected questions only.

Questions marked with an asterisk (*) are the most personally demanding and should be treated as optional disclosures rather than expected contributions in a group setting. They are included because the book modelled the kind of honesty they require, and some readers will want the space to match it.

There are no correct answers. There are honest ones. The distinction is the guide's only standard.

Movement One — The Question
Chapters 1–4

The first four chapters establish the investigation's territory: the nature of collapse, the distinction between feeling suicidal and having suicidal thoughts, the question that most people avoid, and the moment the question turns toward exit. These chapters ask the reader to sit with the question before attempting to answer it.

Questions

1. The book opens with the observation that collapse is not always dramatic or visible — that a person can appear functional while internally struggling to understand why they are still living at all. Have you encountered this gap — in yourself or in someone close to you — between what is visible and what is actually being carried?

Note: This question establishes whether the reader recognises the book's territory from their own experience. It does not require disclosure of personal crisis — the observation about others is an equally valid entry point. In a group setting, it tends to surface quickly whether the book has been read from inside the question or from a safer distance.

2. The book distinguishes between feeling suicidal and having suicidal thoughts — describing the first as an emotional state that does not respond to reasoning, and the second as a cognitive process that can in principle be challenged. Had you encountered this distinction before reading the book? Does it correspond to anything in your own experience or observation?

Note: This is the book's most clinically important contribution and one of its most personally resonant. Many readers will have experienced the emotional form without the cognitive form and will have found themselves unrecognised by frameworks calibrated to detect the cognitive form. This question surfaces that gap and gives it language.

3. Chapter 3 argues that the question Why stay alive? is routinely avoided, suppressed, or quickly answered with familiar reassurances — and that those reassurances often do not meet the question at the level it is being asked. What familiar reassurances have you encountered? Which, if any, have actually helped?

Note: This question distinguishes between responses that reach the question and responses that manage it. It tends to generate honest conversation about the limits of well-intentioned support — from friends, family, and sometimes professionals. The follow-up — which ones actually helped — prevents the conversation from becoming purely critical.

4. Chapter 3 draws a distinction between life containing good things and life being meaningful enough to continue. These are treated as routinely conflated but categorically different. Do you find this distinction real? Can you identify a moment when the first was true and the second felt genuinely uncertain?

Note: This question tests whether the book's central analytical distinction lands as real for the reader. It is more intellectually demanding than the previous questions and works better with readers who have had time to sit with the text. It often produces the most precise and honest answers in a group setting.

5. Chapter 4 argues that the impulse toward exit is often rooted not in a desire for death but in a need to end an unbearable experience — and that this distinction changes what is actually being sought. Does this reframing correspond to anything you have observed or experienced? Does it change how you understand the impulse?

Note: This is the book's most important reframing and the one most likely to be received with resistance by readers from traditions that treat suicidal impulse as primarily moral or spiritual in character. The question is designed to hold the reframing open for examination rather than assertion.

6. Chapter 4 describes the silence that surrounds the consideration of exit — the gap between what is felt and what can be said, and the way that gap is maintained because speaking honestly generates responses calibrated to the wrong statement. Has this silence been part of your own experience or observation? What would have made it easier to speak?

Note: This is the first question that directly invites personal disclosure of the book's most sensitive territory. It is marked as optional in a group setting. Individually, it tends to be the question readers sit with longest. The second part — what would have made it easier to speak — is the more generative half and can stand alone if the first feels too exposed.

7*. The book's Author's Note describes the author writing not from the other side of the question but from inside it — as a last-ditch attempt to find out whether an anchor exists. Did knowing this change how you read the investigation? Does the author's position — still inside the question — affect whether you trust what the book found?

Note: This question addresses the reader's relationship to the author's authority. It is particularly useful for readers who are sceptical of the investigation's conclusion — it separates the question of whether the search was honest from the question of whether the finding is correct, which is a distinction worth making explicit.

Movement Two — The Search Through Modern Anchors
Chapters 5–10

Chapters 5 through 10 examine the anchors most immediately available in contemporary life — pleasure, achievement, relationships, identity, control, and escape — and find each of them genuinely valuable and genuinely insufficient. The movement's organising question is not whether these things matter but whether any of them can carry the full weight of the question under the specific conditions the book is examining.

Questions

1. The book examines six modern anchors across these chapters: pleasure, achievement, relationships, identity, control, and escape. Before reading the investigation's findings, which of these would you have named as your primary anchor — the thing that, more than any other, has made continuing feel justifiable? Did the chapter examining it change how you understand its limits?

Note: This question establishes the reader's personal relationship to the anchor sequence before engaging the investigation's findings. It tends to produce specific, honest answers and creates the basis for the subsequent questions in this movement. In a group setting, it surfaces the diversity of what people rely on and prevents the conversation from assuming a common starting point.

2. Chapter 5 argues that pleasure shifts, under sustained pressure, from being something that enriches life to something that must be maintained in order for life to feel bearable — and that this shift changes its character from a reason for living to a condition for tolerating it. Have you experienced this shift? What did it feel like when it occurred?

Note: This question targets the specific psychological movement the chapter identifies — the moment an enrichment becomes a dependency. It is more personally searching than a general discussion of pleasure's limits and tends to produce more honest and more specific responses as a result.

3. Chapter 6 introduces the question: Am I enough if I stop doing? — and describes this as a question rarely asked directly but frequently lived. Is this a question you recognise? In what contexts has it been most present?

Note: This is the chapter's most emotionally resonant question and the one most likely to surface the specific anxiety of worth tied to output. It is particularly relevant for high-achieving readers, for people who have experienced loss of function through illness or circumstances, and for anyone from a tradition that closely links worth with contribution.

4. Chapter 7 describes the burden inversion — the way that sustained internal distress can convert the relationships that are supposed to anchor a person into responsibilities that must be managed and protected from the full weight of what is being carried. Have you experienced this inversion? What did it do to the relationships involved?

Note: This is the movement's most emotionally demanding question and is marked as requiring care in a group setting. The burden inversion is one of the book's most original insights and one of the most widely recognised by readers who have experienced sustained distress. It surfaces the relational cost of long-term struggle in a way that is rarely named.

5. Chapter 8 examines how identity — including ideological identity — can constrain access to help, using Martin Luther King Jr.'s refusal of psychiatric referral as the clearest available historical example of an identity anchor actively preventing the person it was supposed to sustain from seeking support. Are there identities you hold — professional, communal, spiritual, or otherwise — that have made it harder to acknowledge struggle or seek help?

Note: This question applies the chapter's argument directly to the reader's own identity context. It is particularly relevant for people in public or professional roles, for people from faith traditions with strong norms around strength and spiritual sufficiency, and for anyone whose community's expectations have shaped what they can and cannot disclose.

6. Chapter 9 redefines the anchor standard — arguing that there is a critical difference between what stabilises a person and what remains when stabilisation is no longer enough. Using this distinction, what in your own life has functioned as stabilisation, and what — if anything — has functioned as something deeper?

Note: This question applies the chapter's central analytical contribution directly to the reader's experience. It is one of the most generative questions in the guide because it requires the reader to make a distinction they may not have previously made — between the things that have helped them continue and the things that have given them a reason to.

7. Chapter 10 argues that escape works by interruption — and that interruption is not the same as transformation, so what is not transformed remains. What forms of escape have you used under pressure? Looking back, what did the escape interrupt — and what did it leave unchanged?

Note: This question invites honest reflection on the specific forms escape has taken without requiring the reader to identify them as problematic. The second half — what did it leave unchanged — is the more generative part and brings the investigation's argument to bear on personal experience without moralising about the escape itself.

8. Across these six chapters, the investigation finds each anchor genuinely valuable and genuinely insufficient. Which finding was most difficult to accept — not intellectually, but personally? Which anchor did you most want the investigation to find sufficient?

Note: This question surfaces the reader's emotional investment in the anchor sequence and tends to produce the most honest answers in the movement. It is particularly useful as a closing question for this section because it names the personal stakes of the investigation rather than its intellectual conclusions.

Movement Three — The Frameworks
Chapters 11–12

Chapters 11 and 12 examine the more deliberate responses to the question — meaning frameworks (including Stoic philosophy, existentialist thought, and non-Western traditions) and clinical stabilisation. These are the frameworks most commonly offered to people in sustained distress. The movement's organising question is whether deliberate, structured responses to the question can meet what instinctive responses cannot.

Questions

1. Chapter 11 examines Stoicism's central distinction between what is and is not within one's control, and finds it genuinely useful for reducing unnecessary suffering but insufficient for answering why one should continue when suffering does not resolve. Have you used Stoic principles — formally or informally — as a way of managing difficulty? Where have you found them most useful, and where have they reached their limit?

Note: This question is accessible to readers who have encountered Stoicism through popular culture as well as those with more formal philosophical engagement. The key is the second half — where they have reached their border — which applies the chapter's argument directly to the reader's experience rather than asking for a general assessment of Stoicism's value.

2. Chapter 11 examines the existentialist position that meaning is not found but made — that a person can choose a purpose and commit to it. The investigation finds this position genuinely powerful but ultimately contingent: what is constructed can be reconstructed, what is chosen can be unchosen. Have you built a self-constructed sense of purpose? What has it provided, and where has its contingency become visible?

Note: This question is particularly relevant for readers from secular backgrounds who have invested significantly in personal purpose as an anchor. The contingency observation — what is built can be dismantled — is the chapter's most challenging finding for this group and tends to produce the most searching responses.

3. Chapter 11 notes that both Stoicism and existentialism are primarily cognitive architectures — they require mental clarity to construct, discipline to maintain, and effort to apply. The investigation argues that certain forms of sustained distress are sub-cognitive in origin and therefore beyond the operational range of cognitive frameworks. Does this distinction correspond to your experience of either your own distress or someone else's?

Note: This is the chapter's most important analytical contribution and the most likely to be personally resonant for readers who have found that thinking differently, reframing, or applying philosophical principles has not reached what they are carrying. It gives language to an experience that is frequently made to feel like a failure of will or application.

4. Chapter 12 argues that clinical stabilisation — therapy, medication, structured support — is genuinely valuable and genuinely insufficient as an ultimate anchor. It distinguishes between stabilisation as a survival mechanism and stabilisation as an answer to why survival is worth it. How has clinical support functioned in your own experience or observation? Has it stabilised without answering?

Note: This question requires care in a group setting. It is not intended to discourage clinical help-seeking — the book explicitly endorses it throughout. Its purpose is to surface the distinction between two different things clinical support can and cannot do, which is important for readers who have found clinical support helpful but incomplete.

5. Chapter 12 uses Martin Luther King Jr.'s refusal of psychiatric referral as an example of how public identity can make clinical stabilisation structurally inaccessible. Are there ways in which your identity — communal, professional, spiritual, or otherwise — has affected your relationship to clinical support? Has seeking or accepting it carried a cost?

Note: This question applies the chapter's identity-cost argument to the reader's own context. It is particularly relevant for readers from communities with strong norms around self-sufficiency, spiritual adequacy, or the stigma of mental health treatment. It tends to surface the specific costs that have shaped the reader's relationship to clinical support more precisely than a general question about stigma.

6. The book makes a distinction in Chapter 12 between what stabilises the mind and what gives the mind a reason for its own stabilisation. In your own experience, what has provided each of these? Have they ever been the same thing?

Note: This is the movement's most searching question and the one that most directly bridges the frameworks examined in this movement and the anchor examined in the later chapters. It invites the reader to identify whether they have experienced something that did both, which tends to point toward whatever the reader's own version of the anchor might be.

Movement Four — The Ancient Witnesses and The Defiance of Remaining
Chapters 13–15

Chapters 13 through 15 make two related moves. The first is to widen the investigation's scope — from the contemporary frameworks that have all reached their border — toward the historical record of how human beings have previously engaged with the same question. The second is to name what has actually held for the author across the investigation's biographical span: not a noble anchor but a defiant, unglamorous refusal to concede. Both moves are important for what follows.

Questions

1. Chapter 13 argues that discovering the question has been asked before — by people in different times and cultures — performs a specific psychological function: it de-isolates. The sense that one is carrying something entirely private and unprecedented is changed by the recognition that others have stood in the same place. Has reading this book — or any other — performed this function for you? What changed when you found that the question had already been named?

Note: This question addresses one of the guide's most important therapeutic functions — the de-isolation that historical recognition provides. It is accessible to all readers regardless of their relationship to the book's eventual conclusion, and tends to produce honest conversation about the experience of feeling alone inside a question.

2. Chapter 14 examines four ancient texts — Ecclesiastes, Job, Psalms, and 2 Corinthians — not as doctrine but as witnesses: documents produced by serious people under genuine pressure who took the question all the way to its end. Which of these four witnesses corresponded most closely to your own experience of the question? Which surprised you most?

Note: This question is accessible to readers from faith backgrounds and to secular readers through the scholarly mediation the chapter provides — Harold Bloom on Ecclesiastes, Carl Jung on Job, C.S. Lewis on Psalms, Gabriel Marcel on 2 Corinthians. It does not require prior religious knowledge. The second half — which surprised you most — tends to produce the most generative responses.

3. Chapter 14 presents 2 Corinthians 4:8-9 as the most precise ancient description of what the investigation has been looking for: pressed but not crushed, perplexed but not driven to despair. This is not a description of suffering's removal but of something holding within it. Does this distinction — between suffering's removal and something holding within it — correspond to anything in your own experience of what has helped?

Note: This question introduces the book's central theological finding at the experiential rather than doctrinal level. It is the most important question in this movement for readers who are approaching the faith anchor with scepticism, because it invites them to identify the phenomenon from their own experience before engaging the investigation's name for it.

4. Chapter 15 names what has actually held for the author across the decades of the investigation: not a noble anchor but defiance — the refusal to hand enemies a cheap victory, the anxiety to optimally please a God he is convinced exists, the live against principle when the live for has temporarily failed. Is defiance a form of remaining you recognise? Has it ever been what kept you here when nothing else was sufficient?

Note: This question directly engages the book's most personally honest disclosure and the one most likely to be received with recognition by readers who have survived through stubbornness rather than meaning. It is marked as requiring care in a group setting because the honest answer may involve material the reader has not previously named as a survival mechanism.

5. The book proposes the principle: if you cannot find what to live for, find what you refuse to live for. This is presented not as a philosophy of flourishing but as a philosophy of remaining — sufficient to keep the search alive long enough for something else to reach it. Have you ever lived by this principle, whether or not you named it as such? What were you refusing to concede?

***Note:** This question is the most globally portable in the guide — accessible to readers from every cultural, spiritual, and ideological background because the defiance posture does not require any particular theological commitment. It tends to surface very specific and honest answers about what has actually kept people alive in the absence of more elevated reasons.*

6. Chapter 13 argues that the ancient witnesses are useful not because they resolved the question but because they refused to answer it cheaply — and that this refusal is itself a form of intellectual integrity that the investigation has been trying to match. Looking back across the book's nineteen chapters, do you think the investigation kept that standard? Were there places where you felt it was reaching for a resolution before the search had earned it?

***Note:** This question invites honest critical assessment of the book's investigative integrity — including the possibility that the resistance protocol was not always perfectly maintained. It is particularly useful for readers who are sceptical of the book's conclusion and need space to name that scepticism as a legitimate response to the investigation rather than a failure to receive it.*

7. Chapter 15 discloses that the author once spent time in London signing consent forms for First-in-Human clinical trials — not as a desire for death but as a calculus in which his body's risk felt more valuable than his continuation, and which he recognised later as Joiner's perceived burdensomeness made biographical. Has the weight of being alive ever felt, to you, like more of a cost than a contribution? What changed that calculus, if it did?

***Note:** This is the guide's most sensitive question and the one requiring the most care in a group setting. It is included because the book modelled this level of disclosure, and some readers will want the space to match it. It should never be posed as an expectation and* *should always be preceded by the facilitator naming the crisis resources available. In individual reflection, it can be among the most important questions the guide offers.*

Movement Five — The Anchor
Chapters 16–19 and Epilogue

The final movement examines what the investigation found — the pattern of encounter across different lives and centuries, the five tests applied to the anchor, the biographical redemption of what has held across the author's own search, and the naming of what the investigation identified. The movement's questions do not assume the reader has arrived at the same finding. They assume only that the reader has followed the investigation honestly and is willing to engage its conclusion on its own terms.

Questions

1. Chapter 16 examines three accounts — Pascal, C.S. Lewis, and Francis Collins — of individuals with strong intellectual credentials for dismissing what they encountered and subsequently found they could not. What made these accounts compelling or unconvincing to you? Did the intellectual standing of the witnesses affect how you received what they described?

Note: This question addresses the evidential basis for the investigation's finding before the finding is named. It is designed to separate the question of whether the witnesses are credible from the question of whether what they encountered is real, which is a distinction worth making explicitly, particularly for sceptical readers.

2. Chapter 17 names the anchor as Jesus Christ and examines the claim I am the way, the truth, and the life not as a doctrinal position to be adopted but as a specific claim to be tested against the established standard. How did you receive the naming? Did it feel earned by the investigation — arrived at through the search — or imported from outside it?

Note: This is the guide's most important single question because it addresses the investigation's central integrity claim: that the conclusion was found rather than predetermined. The distinction between arrived at through the search and imported into it is the resistance protocol's defining test, and the reader's honest assessment of whether the book passed it is more valuable than any prescribed response.

3. Chapter 18 applies five tests to Jesus Christ as an anchor — historical grounding, psychological reduction, durability under collapse, dependence or independence, and limits. Which test did you find most rigorous? Which did you feel was handled least adequately? Are there tests you would have applied that the chapter did not?

Note: This question invites critical engagement with the chapter's methodology rather than its conclusion. It is particularly useful for readers with philosophical or scientific backgrounds who engage more readily with the quality of the examination than with the examined claim. Honest answers about which tests were handled least adequately are more valuable to the investigation than polite endorsements of all five.

4. Chapter 18 argues that a person cannot be tested from a distance — that the test of whether Jesus Christ holds as an anchor requires proximity rather than analysis alone. It closes with the question: Will I come close enough to find out — close enough to the person the investigation has named, Jesus Christ, to test what cannot be tested from a distance? Where are you with that question? Has the investigation brought you to a threshold you had not previously stood at?

Note: This is the guide's most personally searching question and the one most likely to produce silence before speech, which is the right response. It does not require an answer in any particular direction. It requires only honesty about where the reader actually is, which is the same standard the book applied to itself throughout.

5. The Epilogue names the anchor without qualification — His name is Jesus Christ — and uses Matthew 11:28 as its centre of gravity: Come unto me, all ye that labour and are heavy laden, and I will give you rest. For a reader still inside the question, what does that invitation feel like? Accessible? Conditional? Too simple? Too demanding? Something else entirely?

Note: This question invites the reader to engage with the invitation on its own terms rather than as a theological proposition. The range of responses — accessible, conditional, too simple, too demanding — is all valid entry points into the conversation. The question is designed to surface where the reader's resistance or openness actually lives, which is more useful than a general assessment of whether the invitation is true.

6. The final chapter closes with three addresses to the reader: one for those who found nothing that holds, one for those who recognised something that might hold, and one for those who remain uncertain. Which address was yours? Has that position changed in the course of reading — or in the course of this conversation?

Note: This question provides a natural closing point for the movement and for the guide as a whole. It returns the reader to the book's most generous passage and invites honest self-location within it. The second half — has that position changed — is the more valuable question and should be given the most time if the group is near the end of its session.

7. The book describes its own position in the Author's Note as a last-ditch attempt to find out whether an anchor exists — written not from the other side of the question but from inside it. Having read the investigation, do you think the author found what he was looking for? And separately: did you?

Note: This is the guide's final question and the one that returns the investigation to its origin — the Author's Note's honest statement of what the book was attempting. The two halves — did the author find it, and did you — are deliberately separated because the answers may be different, and that difference is worth naming. The guide closes here, not because the search is over, but because the question is now yours to carry forward.

A Closing Note

The investigation is complete. However, the conversation it has generated — in this guide, in the groups and individuals who have used it, in the private reflection of readers who have followed the question honestly — is not.

If you have arrived at this point still inside the question, you are not behind. You are in the same place the author was when he wrote the Author's Note. The search is worth continuing. The anchor of the investigation does not require the search to be finished before He's approached. It requires only the smallest available honest movement toward Him.

Endnotes

Chapter 1 — *When Life Implodes*

1. William Styron, *Darkness Visible: A Memoir of Madness*, 1990.

2. For a clinical framework distinguishing emotional dysregulation from suicidal ideation, see Matthew K. Nock et al., *"Suicide and Suicidal Behaviour,"* Epidemiologic Reviews, 2008.

[3] Viktor Frankl, *Man's Search for Meaning*, 1946.

Chapter 2 — *When Despair Takes Different Forms*

1. Edwin Shneidman, *The Suicidal Mind*, 1996. Shneidman coined the term *psychache* to describe unbearable psychological pain as the primary driver of suicidal *crisis* — *distinct from ideation or plan.*

2. *Aaron T. Beck et al., "The Measurement of Pessimism: The Hopelessness Scale,"* Journal of Consulting and Clinical Psychology, 1974. Beck's cognitive model of suicidality, centred on hopelessness as the key cognitive variable, remains foundational to clinical assessment.

Chapter 3 — *The Question Most People Avoid*

1. Albert Camus, *The Myth of Sisyphus*, 1942. The full opening: *"There is but one truly serious philosophical problem, and that is suicide."* Camus ultimately argued against suicide — not on moral grounds but on the grounds that revolt against the absurd requires a living subject. Still, the framing of the question itself remains the most direct philosophical treatment of this book's central inquiry.

2. The distinction between happiness, pleasure, and meaning as separate categories of human flourishing is examined in Susan Wolf, *Meaning in Life and Why It Matters*, 2010. Wolf argues that a meaningful life requires engagement with something beyond one's own subjective satisfaction—a framework that directly explains why conventional answers to despair often fail to achieve it.

Chapter 4 — *When the Question Turns Toward Exit*

1. Edwin S. Shneidman, *The Suicidal Mind,* 1996. Shneidman's concept of *psychache* — unbearable psychological pain—reframes suicidal crisis as a pain-relief response rather than a death-seeking one, with significant implications for both clinical intervention and the philosophical investigation this book is undertaking.

2. Thomas Joiner, *Why People Die by Suicide,* 2005. Joiner's Interpersonal Theory of Suicide identifies three converging conditions: thwarted belongingness, perceived burdensomeness, and acquired capability for self-harm. The third element — capability — is particularly relevant here, as it addresses the psychological function of perceived agency in situations of overwhelming internal experience.

3. From the author's documented personal experience. Phase 1 clinical trials — First-in-Human studies — are the earliest stage of human testing for experimental compounds, conducted primarily to establish safety, dosage, and adverse reaction profiles rather than therapeutic efficacy. Healthy volunteers are recruited and compensated. The consent process requires acknowledgement of risks that, by definition, are not fully known. The author's participation in this process during a period of sustained financial and psychological pressure constitutes a biographical instance of the perceived burdensomeness framework identified in endnote 2 above.

Chapter 5 — *What Pleasure Promises*

1. The concept of hedonic adaptation originates with Brickman and Campbell's foundational 1971 essay *"Hedonic Relativism and Planning the Good Society."* Daniel Kahneman's subsequent work — particularly his distinction between *experienced utility* (how an experience feels in the moment) and *remembered utility* (how it is evaluated in retrospect) — extends this framework in ways directly relevant to why pleasurable experience frequently fails to sustain long-term meaning. See Kahneman, *Thinking, Fast and Slow,* 2011.

2. Martin E. P. Seligman, *Flourish,* 2011. Seligman's PERMA model distinguishes positive emotion from meaning, engagement, relationships, and accomplishment as separate contributors to well-being—a framework that resists the conflation of feeling good with living well that this chapter examines.

Chapter 6 — *What Achievement Promises*

1. Edwin A. Locke and Gary P. Latham, *"Building a Practically Useful Theory of Goal Setting and Task Motivation,"* American Psychologist, 2002. Locke and Latham's research demonstrates that specific, challenging goals enhance motivation and

perceived purpose — but their framework also distinguishes between performance goals (output-oriented) and learning goals (development-oriented), a distinction relevant to why achievement tied exclusively to external output tends to produce fragile rather than durable meaning.

2. Leo Tolstoy, *A Confession*, 1882. Written when Tolstoy was in his early fifties, at the height of his literary reputation. The full document is an extended first-person account of arriving at the question of suicide through the failure of achievement, family, fame, and faith to provide sufficient grounds for continuation — and constitutes perhaps the most honest extended treatment of this book's central question by any major literary figure.

Chapter 7 — *What Relationships Promise*

1. John T. Cacioppo and William Patrick, *Loneliness: Human Nature and the Need for Social Connection*, 2008. Cacioppo's neurological and psychological research established that social connection functions as a biological need, not merely a preference — its absence producing measurable physiological stress responses comparable to physical pain.

2. From the author's documented personal experience of living with sustained suicidal feelings without suicidal ideation — a distinction that consistently exceeded the available clinical and relational frameworks for communication. The gap between experience and language is not unique to this condition, but is particularly acute within it.

3. Julianne Holt-Lunstad et al., *"Loneliness and Social Isolation as Risk Factors for Mortality,"* Perspectives on Psychological Science, 2015. Holt-Lunstad's meta-analysis of 148 studies found that perceived loneliness — the subjective gap between desired and achieved connection — was a stronger predictor of mortality than objective social isolation. This finding reframes loneliness as an internal experience rather than a social circumstance.

4. C.S. Lewis, *A Grief Observed*, 1961. Written in the immediate aftermath of his wife Joy Davidman's death from cancer. The journal was initially published under a pseudonym; Lewis later acknowledged authorship. It remains the most unguarded account of the collapse of relational anchoring through loss by any major twentieth-century writer.

5. Thomas Joiner, *Why People Die by Suicide*, 2005. Joiner's concept of perceived burdensomeness — introduced in Chapter 4 in the context of agency — finds its most direct application here, in the relational context for which it was primarily developed.

Chapter 8 — *What Identity and Ideology Promise*

1. Erik Erikson, Identity: Youth and Crisis, 1968. Erikson's framework of psychosocial development — particularly his concept of identity as an ongoing negotiation rather than a fixed achievement — provides the foundational clinical understanding of why identity shifts, fractures, and requires both internal coherence and external recognition to remain stable.

2. Henri Tajfel and John Turner, *"An Integrative Theory of Intergroup Conflict,"* 1979. Social Identity Theory's core finding — that individuals derive significant self-concept and resilience from group membership — explains both the strength of ideological anchoring and the specific vulnerability that emerges when group belonging is disrupted, or the group's framework is challenged.

3. Arthur Koestler, contribution to Richard Crossman, ed. *The God That Failed*, 1949. Six intellectuals — including Koestler, Ignazio Silone, André Gide, and Richard Wright — documented the arc of commitment to and disillusionment with communism. Koestler's account remains the most analytically precise description of what happens when an ideological framework encounters the lived experience it cannot account for.

4. The 1967 dining table scene is documented in Nassir Ghaemi, A First-Rate Madness: Uncovering the Links Between Leadership and Mental Illness, 2011, and in the accounts of Clarence Jones, who was present. Ghaemi's broader analysis of King's depressive episodes — drawing on medical records, correspondence, and testimony from those closest to him — provides the primary scholarly documentation of King's psychological history and its relationship to his public identity.

Chapter 9 — *What Control and Regulation Provide*

1. Stephen Porges, *The Polyvagal Theory*, 2011. Porges's framework explains how the autonomic nervous system — particularly the vagal pathways — mediates between physiological states and felt safety. His work provides the neurological basis for understanding why embodied practices such as regulated breathing, movement, and rhythm can produce genuine emotional stabilisation independently of cognitive intervention.

2. From the author's documented personal experience — specifically, the distinction between the emotional state of feeling suicidal and the cognitive state of having suicidal thoughts. The pressure described as *emotional encasement* is a sustained, non-cognitive state that does not respond to the reasoning-based

interventions typically applied to suicidal ideation. This distinction, central to the author's memoir, is clinically underrecognised.

3. From the author's documented experience of sustained emotional pressure affecting daily functioning — decisions feeling impossible, ordinary activities becoming effortful, the floor of daily experience requiring active maintenance rather than being taken for granted.

4. Irvin D. Yalom, *Existential Psychotherapy*, 1980. Yalom's four ultimate concerns — death, freedom, isolation, and meaninglessness — frame the existential dimension of psychological distress as categorically distinct from its symptomatic dimension. His clinical observation that symptom relief does not generate meaning is foundational to the chapter's central distinction.

5. Viktor Frankl, *Man's Search for Meaning*, 1946. Frankl's concept of *noögenic neurosis* — existential distress arising specifically from a failure to find meaning rather than from psychological disorder — establishes the clinical and philosophical basis for understanding why the question of *why continue?* cannot be adequately addressed by stabilisation alone.

Chapter 10 — *When Escape Becomes an Anchor*

1. Bessel van der Kolk, *The Body Keeps the Score*, 2014. Van der Kolk's research into trauma and the nervous system establishes that avoidance responses to overwhelming experience are neurologically automatic rather than consciously chosen — a finding with direct implications for how escape behaviours should be understood clinically and, more broadly, in any honest account of human responses to sustained internal pressure.

2. William Styron, *Darkness Visible*, 1990. Styron's account of alcohol as a decades-long management tool — and its sudden failure at sixty — provides the most precisely documented available narrative of escape becoming structural and then catastrophically insufficient. His description of what arrived when the buffer was removed is among the most honest accounts of sustained depressive weight in the literary record.

3. Anna Lembke, *Dopamine Nation*, 2021. Lembke's clinical and neurological account of how repeated engagement in reward-seeking and numbing behaviours creates reinforcing loops — short-term relief strengthening the impulse to return while underlying conditions remain unchanged — provides the behavioural science framework for understanding why escape cycles persist independently of conscious intention.

4. From the author's documented personal experience — specifically, the sustained and enduring rather than episodic nature of the emotional state: feelings that persisted across long periods and intense episodes, a cycle of emotional pain that did not resolve with the passage of time. This thread of the memoir documents the specific quality of the experience that makes any form of interruption comprehensible as a response.

5. From the author's documented experience of the emotional state's resistance to cognitive intervention, the sustained pressure that does not argue or reason and therefore cannot be addressed through reasoning alone. The distinction between interruption and transformation emerges directly from the lived experience of a state that interrupts without resolving.

Chapter 11 — *What Meaning Frameworks Attempt*

1. Aaron T. Beck, *Cognitive Therapy and the Emotional Disorders*, 1976. Beck's foundational work established that cognitive appraisal — the interpretation of events — significantly determines emotional responses. This finding drew explicitly on Stoic philosophical principles and remains the basis of cognitive behavioural therapy.

2. Marcus Aurelius, *Meditations*, written c. 161–180 CE, published posthumously. The *Meditations* were written as a private philosophical journal — never intended for publication — making them among the most unguarded accounts available of how the Stoic framework was actually applied to a life under sustained pressure, rather than merely theorised in the abstract.

3. From the author's documented personal experience — specifically, the observation that the struggle stems from acute situations and what the author describes as a traumatised subconscious: overwhelming emotional responses tied not to specific logical processes but to triggers that cannot always be discerned or escaped. This experience places the author's struggle in a category that cognitive meaning frameworks are not primarily designed to address — not because the frameworks are inadequate, but because the state being addressed is sub-cognitive in origin.

4. Albert Camus, *Notebooks 1935–1951*, published posthumously. The private notebooks reveal the ongoing tension between the philosophical confidence of Camus's published work and his personal reckoning with whether the framework he had constructed could carry the weight of his own experience, making them a more useful document for this investigation than his formal philosophical essays.

5. For cases of Non-Western meaning frameworks addressing comparable territory, see Thich Nhat Hanh, *The Heart of the Buddha's Teaching*, 1998, for the

Buddhist treatment of suffering, impermanence, and the possibility of meaning in the absence of permanent selfhood. This tradition approaches the investigation's central question from a fundamentally different starting point and reaches conclusions that are not easily mapped onto the Western philosophical frameworks examined here.

Chapter 12 — *Can Stabilising the Mind Give a Reason to Live?*

1. World Health Organisation, *Guidelines for the Management of Physical Health Conditions in Adults with Severe Mental Disorders*, 2018; and the broader evidence base summarised in Pim Cuijpers et al., *"Psychotherapies for Depression: A Network Meta-Analysis,"* World Psychiatry, 2019. The evidence for therapeutic and pharmacological intervention in depressive and anxiety conditions is robust across multiple national and international clinical guidelines, including NICE *Depression in Adults: Treatment and Management* (UK). The convergence across healthcare systems and cultures on the effectiveness of structured intervention strengthens rather than localises the claim.

2. From the author's documented personal experience — medical diagnosis of anxiety and depression, with the struggles predating that diagnosis by decades. The description of therapy sessions as not well-matched to the presenting experience reflects the specific challenge of bringing a sustained, non-cognitive emotional state — the feeling of being suicidal without suicidal ideation — to therapeutic frameworks primarily calibrated for cognitive presentations. This is not a generalised criticism of therapy but an honest account of a specific clinical gap that is increasingly recognised in the literature on affective disorders.

3. King's refusal of Dr Arthur Logan's psychiatric referral in late 1967 is documented in Nassir Ghaemi's A First-Rate Madness (2011. The broader pattern of identity cost as a barrier to clinical help-seeking is examined in Patrick Corrigan's "How Stigma Interferes with Mental Health Care," American Psychologist, 2004 — a foundational paper on the relationship between public identity, perceived stigma, and the decision not to seek available clinical support.

4. For the clinical recognition of this gap, see Matthew Nock et al., *"Suicide and Suicidal Behaviour,"* Epidemiologic Reviews, 2008 — previously cited in Chapter 2 — which notes the persistent difficulty in clinical assessment of suicidal risk in individuals presenting with affective rather than ideational symptoms. The author's experience represents a clinically documented presentation that standard frameworks do not always adequately reach.

5. William Styron, *Darkness Visible*, 1990. Styron's account of his hospitalisation and the unexpected musical moment that preceded his recovery is among the

most precise descriptions available of the distinction between clinical stabilisation as a survival condition and the separate, unaccounted-for arrival of whatever makes survival meaningful. His inability to explain what the music did — only that it did something the clinical environment had not — is the honest limit of his account, and it is precisely that honesty that makes it useful here.

Chapter 13 — *Have We Been Here Before?*

1. William Barrett, *Irrational Man: A Study in Existential Philosophy*, 1958. Barrett's survey of existential thought across Western philosophical history — from ancient Greece through the twentieth century — documents the persistent recurrence of the question of existence's justification as a practical rather than merely theoretical concern, present across radically different cultural and historical contexts.

2. Leo Tolstoy, *A Confession*, 1882. Tolstoy's account of his deliberate turn toward peasant wisdom, ancient texts, and non-Western traditions — after exhausting the frameworks available to his educated class — is the most precisely documented available narrative of the turn this chapter is describing: from the exhaustion of modern frameworks toward the historical record, motivated not by nostalgia but by the recognition that the question deserved older witnesses.

3. Pierre Hadot, *Philosophy as a Way of Life*, 1995. Hadot's foundational argument — that ancient philosophical traditions were practical responses to the question of how to live rather than primarily theoretical systems — reframes the entire ancient philosophical record as a sustained, serious engagement with the question this investigation is pursuing. His concept of *spiritual exercises* as philosophical practice is directly relevant to the investigation's focus on ancient wisdom traditions.

4. For the psychological literature on temporal self-expansion and its relationship to perceived isolation, see Dan P. McAdams, *The Stories We Live By*, 1993. McAdams's narrative identity framework suggests that locating one's own experience within a larger historical or cultural story significantly affects the subjective experience of that story's weight — a finding with direct relevance to why historical witness performs a de-isolating function that contemporary frameworks cannot replicate.

Chapter 14 — *The Brutal Honesty of Ancient Wisdom*

1. Harold Bloom, *The Western Canon*, 1994. Bloom's assessment of Ecclesiastes as the most genuinely sceptical book in the biblical canon — and one of the most honest in the Western literary tradition — frames the text as a literary and

philosophical document that secular readers can engage on its own terms, independently of its religious reception.

2. The Book of Ecclesiastes, authorship and date debated, conventionally placed between the 5th and 2nd centuries BCE. The Hebrew term *hevel* — rendered as *vanity* in most English translations — is more precisely understood as *breath* or *vapour,* naming the quality of impermanence rather than moral worthlessness. This distinction is central to the text's relevance to this investigation.

3. Marcus Aurelius, *Meditations,* c. 161–180 CE. The convergence between Aurelius's Stoic conclusions and Ecclesiastes' observations — reached through entirely different intellectual traditions separated by several centuries — constitutes a form of cross-cultural evidential confirmation that neither text alone could provide.

4. Carl Jung, *Answer to Job,* 1952. Jung's psychological engagement with the Book of Job — controversial precisely because it treated the text as a serious psychological document rather than devotional literature — identifies Job's refusal to accept the explanatory frameworks offered by his community as the text's most important intellectual moment. Jung's reading is relevant here not as a theological endorsement but as the most rigorous secular psychological engagement with the text in the twentieth century.

5. C.S. Lewis, *Reflections on the Psalms,* 1958. Lewis's literary and psychological analysis of the Psalms — written as a scholar engaging with ancient poetry rather than as a devotional commentary — identifies their emotional oscillation as a feature rather than a flaw: the honest account of an interior life that does not maintain consistent positions under sustained pressure.

6. Gabriel Marcel, *Being and Having,* 1949. Marcel's philosophical distinction between optimism — a disposition toward improving conditions — and hope — a persistence that conditions cannot reach — provides the closest secular philosophical parallel to what the 2 Corinthians passage is describing. Marcel arrived at this distinction through phenomenological philosophy; Paul arrived at it through lived experience. The convergence is the evidentiary point of the investigation.

Chapter 15 — *The Defiance of Remaining*

1. Albert Camus, *The Myth of Sisyphus,* 1942. Camus's concept of revolt — the defiant, conscious refusal to accept the absurd as the final word — is the secular philosophical framework most directly parallel to the defiance position this chapter is examining. Importantly, Camus explicitly rejected suicide as a response to the absurd precisely on these grounds: that it concedes to the absurd rather

than refusing it. His position is not identical to the chapter's — he does not share its theological dimension — but it confirms that living against, in the absence of living for, is a philosophically coherent and historically documented response to this investigation's central question.

2. Winston Churchill's depression is documented in William Manchester, *The Last Lion: Winston Spencer Churchill*, Vol. 1, 1983, and in Churchill's own correspondence. Manchester's account of Churchill's private struggles — and the role of defiant opposition to external enemies in sustaining his will through periods of severe depressive episodes — is the most accessible historical parallel to the chapter's argument about oppositional motivation as a survival mechanism.

3. Viktor E. Frankl, *Man's Search for Meaning*, 1946. Frankl documents how survival under extreme conditions was sustained, in many cases, by resistance and refusal before positive meaning was fully formed. It is important to note, however, that Frankl's framework ultimately requires the formation of meaning to complete the survival arc — a requirement that the chapter's investigation identifies as precisely the point at which defiance alone reaches its limit, and the search must continue.

Chapter 16 — *When Something Begins to Hold*

1. Blaise Pascal, *Memorial*, 1654. The document — discovered sewn into Pascal's coat only after he died in 1662 — is among the most precisely documented records of an experiential encounter available from the Western intellectual tradition. Its significance lies not only in its content but in Pascal's decision to keep it private and physical: a record carried on the body rather than published or performed, suggesting a relationship to the experience that exceeded what public discourse could accommodate.

2. C.S. Lewis, *Surprised by Joy*, 1955. Lewis's autobiography of his intellectual and experiential journey toward belief is notable for its consistent emphasis on the encounter's unsolicited character — his repeated description of finding himself confronted by something he had not sought and could not, on examination, dismiss. His account in Chapter 14 of Surprised by Joy — describing the moment of conversion as occurring in a vehicle travelling between Whipsnade and Oxford — is deliberately unromantic, resisting the narrative conventions of religious experience in favour of honest description.

3. Francis Collins, *The Language of God*, 2006. Collins's account of his conversion — from the position of a scientist who considered belief intellectually untenable to a person who found himself unable to sustain that position after sustained examination — is the most credible contemporary parallel to Pascal's account. His scientific standing provides the evidential standard that makes the account useful

to the investigation: a person professionally committed to the quality of evidence, applying that commitment to the question of what he encountered, and finding the encounter survived the examination.

4. Lewis R. Rambo, *Understanding Religious Conversion*, 1993. Rambo's cross-cultural study of conversion — drawing on psychological, sociological, and anthropological frameworks — documents the consistent pattern of crisis, encounter, and transformation that exceeds purely rational progression across diverse cultural and historical contexts. His framework confirms that what this chapter is observing is not an anomaly but a recurrence, and provides the scholarly mediation between the individual accounts and the investigation's broader claim.

Chapter 17 — *When the Anchor Is No Longer Avoided*

1. Taylor Branch, *Parting the Waters: America in the King Years 1954–1963*, 1988; and Martin Luther King Jr., *Stride Toward Freedom*, 1958. King's account of the kitchen table prayer — and the specific quality of what arrived in response — is documented in both sources. Branch's historical account provides the broader context of the crisis that preceded the moment; King's own account provides the experiential description. The moment is dated January 27, 1956.

2. Habakkuk 3:17–18, King James Version. The passage in full: *"Although the fig tree shall not blossom, neither shall fruit be in the vines; the labour of the olive shall fail, and the fields shall yield no meat; the flock shall be cut off from the fold, and there shall be no herd in the stalls: yet I will rejoice in the Lord, I will joy in the God of my salvation."* Written from within conditions of sustained national crisis and the complete absence of visible grounds for hope. The text's value to this investigation lies not in its theological conclusions but in its grammatical structure: the *yet* that holds without requiring the conditions to first resolve.

3. Gospel of John 14:6, King James Version. The full verse: *"Jesus saith unto him, I am the way, the truth, and the life: no man cometh unto the Father, but by me."* The investigation engages specifically with the first-person present-tense identity claim — *I am* rather than *I show* or *I give* — as the structural feature that distinguishes this from the framework-based anchors previously examined.

4. Gospel of John 5:40, King James Version, in context of verses 39–40. The structural claim — that life is being sought in what testifies about a person rather than in the person directly — reframes the entire investigative enterprise of this book as a movement toward a specific encounter rather than an accumulation of sufficient information.

Chapter 18 — *Testing the Person Directly*

1. Richard Bauckham, *Jesus and the Eyewitnesses*, 2006. Bauckham's detailed argument — that the Gospel accounts reflect eyewitness testimony rather than legendary development — is based on the analysis of named individuals, the distribution of personal names consistent with first-century Palestinian demographics, and the internal patterns of the accounts themselves. The argument does not prove the theological claims. It establishes that the historical question cannot be dismissed at the level of myth.

2. The accounts of Pascal's *Memorial* (1654), Lewis's *Surprised by Joy* (1955), and King's kitchen table prayer (January 27, 1956) have been examined in detail in previous chapters of this investigation. Their relevance here is specifically to the psychological reduction test: each represents a person with strong intellectual credentials for dismissing what they encountered, who subsequently found that the experience did not dissolve under analytical scrutiny — and who described it consistently in terms of *otherness* rather than internal construction.

3. William James, *The Varieties of Religious Experience*, 1902. James's foundational psychological study of religious encounter — conducted from an explicitly empirical rather than theological standpoint — identifies the sense of *presence* and *otherness* as the most consistent feature of experiential accounts that cannot be fully accounted for by purely internal psychological processes. His framework does not endorse the theological content of such experiences; it documents their phenomenological structure and resists the premature reduction of that structure to known psychological categories.

4. The biographical data referred to here — the sustained emotional weight, the non-resolution of underlying conditions, and the continued operative presence of what Chapter 17 identified as the anchor — constitute the investigation's most direct available evidence for the durability test. It is not a controlled study. It is a thirty-year longitudinal account of a specific person's specific experience, reported with the honesty the investigation has maintained throughout.

For permissions, subsidiary rights, or bulk orders:

ahamigbokwe@outlook.com

www.X.com/iampastoraham